Forged in Fire
Girl on Fire

*A personal journey told through poetry
and journaling*

Elaine Brady, Ph.D.

Forged in Fire — Girl on Fire

Copyright ©2015 by Elaine Brady, Ph.D.

ISBN13: 978-1-61170-166-1
ISBN10: 1-61170-166-X

Library of Congress Control Number: 2014935603

Published by:

 Robertson Publishing™
www.RobertsonPublishing.com

Printed in the USA, UK, and Australia on acid-free paper.

Additional copies of this book are available through:
www.amazon.com
www.barnesandnoble.com

Acknowledgements

I would like to express my great appreciation to those who have supported and guided the creation of this book:

SisterSpirit Retreat and the women who emboldened me to write this book.

Allen, Karen, Mary & Leah, my invaluable critique group.

Parthenia M. Hicks, Editor & Poet Laureate Emerita, Los Gatos, CA, without your unwavering support and guidance this work would not have been "birthed."

Calder Lowe, Award-winning Writer and Executive editor, Dragonfly Press. Your personal and professional input breathed life back into a flagging author.

Denise A. Leffers, MFT, an early reader who offered valuable feedback.

Diane, my ever-positive partner.

INTRODUCTION

The call to write this book flowed, not just from my own story, but from the hundreds of similar stories I have been honored to hear over my thirty years as a therapist. Some of the stories have been told by children, others by adults, but they have all carried the same message—*there is hope.*

How does a young and vulnerable spirit survive emotional, physical, and/or sexual abuse by the very people she looks to for love, nurturance, and protection? What happens when a child suffers this ultimate betrayal of trust and love? Can anyone ever really heal from the most devastating of personal invasions — incest? Tragically, millions of children don't.

Every year in the United States, more than three million reports of child abuse, involving more than six million children, are made in the United States—with between 1,500 to 2,555 children dying as a result of their injuries or neglect.[1] Shockingly, an additional 4,900 choose to end their own lives (1/5 of those are between five and fourteen years old).[2]

Yet, while it is overwhelming and tragic to imagine these children suffering such devastating pain, we can take heart in the fact that many children manage to not just survive, but to actually move forward and thrive. In fact, one notable study found that forty-nine percent of adult survivors of child abuse showed this amazing level of resiliency.[3] Their ability to transform their childhood suffering into a celebration of themselves and of life itself is a powerful testimony to the strength and endurance of the human spirit.

---

[1] U.S. Department of Health and Human Services, Administration for Children and Families, Administration on Children, Youth and Families, Children's Bureau (2013). Child Maltreatment 2012. http://www.acf.hhs.gov/programs/cb/research-data-technology/statistics-research/child-maltreatment

[2] National Vital Statistics Report, Vol. 61, No. 4, May 8, 2013, p 90.

[3] Afifi, T. and MacMillan, H. L. Resilience Following Child Maltreatment: A Review of Protective Factors. Canadian Journal of Psychiatry. May 2011, Vol. 56 Issue 5, p 266 - 272.

This book depicts one such journey of pain and recovery. In it, we share the life of Sammie as she flounders through many difficult years, ever struggling to find healing, happiness and love. While her journey is often painful to share, in doing so we bear witness to the incessant human struggle for understanding and mastery over our lives. And in her recovery, we are reminded that we often cannot fully appreciate the beauty and joy of life until we have experienced its deepest darkness and grief.

Sammie tells us her story in the form of poetry and short stories—a journal in verse—welcoming us into the hidden haven that helped her spirit survive. Her stories are rich with cultural references to a period in American history that often seemed to reflect her own turmoil—the 1960s and 70s. The culture and events of these eras both mirror her own struggles and become a part of them as she strives to navigate her way through life's sometimes treacherous waters.

The flowing and lyrical nature of Sammie's poetry helps to soften the sharp edges of truth often hidden just beneath the surface of those waters, ever drawing us on as we join Sammie's sometimes reckless ride through the wild currents of her life. And, at long last, we sigh with relief and pride as she finally finds safe harbor.

Sammie shares her story, not just for her own sake, but for all the wounded children out there who are still suffering and calling out for help. If you listen with your heart, you may even hear that voice calling from within yourself, *Heal me, I will grow.*

Elaine Brady

Elaine Brady, Ph.D., MFT, CAS, CSAT-S
Executive Director
Net Worth Recovery, Inc.
1190 S. Bascom Ave., Ste. 130
San Jose, CA 95128
1.408.283.9305
networth@networthrecovery.com
http://networthrecovery.com/

Forged in Fire

Girl on Fire

Contents

Voices

FORGED

To you
I am a phantom
as yet a great unknown

A mystery
my beginning
or how it is I've grown

Born
of coldest ice
Born
of hottest flame
Born
with soul unformed
Born
without a name

Hammered on the anvil
thrust into the fire
ravaged and consumed by
His need
His desire

Soul burned down to bone
yet one small ember
shone

Smoldered
Ignited
Grew

Now
there is no end to me
I am the earth
I am the sea

Like a cloud filled sky
I have wept
Like the oceans
I have depth
Like the mountains
I have range
Like the universe
I change

Ever evolving
growing
All about me
rearranging

And yet
I am granite
as constant
as this planet

I have become
All
I am today

Tempered spirit
born
anew

Forged
to show others
The Way

SPEAK FOR ME

"Why am I doing this?" I cry into the night, "Putting pen to paper and pouring out my soul, black letters spilling across the page like inky blood. Dredging up the silted past from the deepest recesses of my soul. Excavating the covered gravesites of each and every wound, just to scoop out the buried memories, raw and hurtful still."

"Why?"I demand. "What unmined wisdom could I possibly unearth that others have not exposed to the light of day before?" Leaden silence weighs heavy on my ears.

"Why!?" I shout my agony into the heartless void.

These tortured questions echoed through the hollow chambers of my heart; swept through a darkened hallway, an empty bedroom and down the unlit cellar stairs. Found at last a hidden child, huddled in the dark. Large sunken eyes in ancient face looked slowly up at me and she whispered, *"Speak for me."*

GHOST CHILD

Have you seen my face before?
Do you know my name?
Can you hear me calling
in a sad refrain?

Will you come to see me?
Will you bring me home?
Will you keep me always
wherever you may roam?

Do I ask too much of you
or do I ask too little
for all the years you've hidden me
your memories grown
dry and brittle?

Did you really think you'd left me
somewhere far behind
even while somehow knowing
Fate pays back in kind?

Please take my hand and love me
never let me go
for I am still a part of you
heal me
I will grow

Home Sweet Home

The impact of the solid hit still reverberated down the long-bone tuning fork of her right arm as Sammie's calloused, dirty feet pounded over first base, charging toward second. The sharp crack of hard ball hitting harder bat sliced through the hot dry Texas air like a bolt of lightning, and the small white orb still sailed high into the clear blue sky.

Her chest swelled with gasping breaths and pride. She was the strongest kid on the block and the only one who could lift the solid cement cap off the sewer drain when a ball rolled into it.

A huge smile lit her densely freckled face as she stole a quick glance over her shoulder and saw the ball bounce into heavy weeds at the back of the playing field. They'd never catch her now! But that didn't slow her all-out race for home base. She relished the feel of her strong legs pounding into the hard-packed earth, her sinewy arms punching the air in counter-rhythm to her feet, the wind of her passage lifting her heavy hair off her sweaty neck. It was the closest she could come to flying.

And her heart was soaring as she hit the soft sand-filled bag of home base for the winning run. Her foot hadn't even cleared the bag before she was swallowed up in the joyful embrace of her teammates, their screams deafening in her ears.

She was twelve and, when not at home, *life was good.*

EMPTY CUP

Like a homeless   pauper
empty shell   and bent
my mother   holds
an empty   cup
every drop   of love
already
s
p
e
n
t

THE ONLY TOUCH

He takes me hunting
fishing too
all the things he lets
my older brothers do
leather working
fixing car
mending roof
with pitch-black tar

And when we go
on family trips
I pretend
to be asleep
just so he'll carry me in

      His
the only touch
    I know

He is my hero
except when mad
then he becomes
something else
not my dad

A wild wolf maybe
or a rabid dog
some hunched-back creature
driven insane
by some Thing
he can never name

For that is when
his razor strop
will fall
again and again
upon my back
my head, my hands
any place
at all

The whole while
my heart fills
with the terror
of not knowing
if or when
it will ever
stop

Pain
shame
humiliation
all rolled into one
just because I made
too much noise
having too much fun

And as I grew
his was the only touch
I knew

KILL ZONE

I slip as quietly as I can
through the front door
of my Home Sweet Home
easing into the living room
I try to tiptoe across the carpet
without letting my feet touch the floor
an old Indian trick Tonto taught
the Lone Ranger

Little brother and sis
lie zombie-like
in front of the TV
oblivious to my passage
big brother sits stiff
on the sagging brown couch
hidden behind
a book

Bang of copper pots
from the kitchen
makes me wonder
what little children
Mother Ogre has ground up
for dinner tonight

Invisible
I avoid her death-ray stare
the dreaded forewarning
of my father's wrath

Silent
I reach the hallway
undetected
fear choking my throat

This is the Kill Zone
the worst two feet to cross
life depending on my parents'
bedroom door being closed

Frozen
not knowing
if the Dragon
is really sleeping
or perched there
just inside

Waiting
to flame me
with his fury
for something I have
or have not
done

Breathing deep
holding my breath
I stretch my too-short legs wide
try hard to bridge
the narrow minefield
of the hall
in just one stride

At long last reaching
  the relative safety
    of my bedroom

The torture chamber
    where I hide

Spiritual Death

HEAVEN'S LIGHT DIES

In the wild exuberance
of youth
I am beaten
into submission

Wings clipped
I plummet
to hard earth

Soon, I forget the joy
of wind in my hair
the feel
of soft clouds beneath my feet

Earthbound
I drag myself through
a mire of hurt and pain
all my world foreshadowed
by dark clouds of fear
Soul broken
by blows
that maim

Heaven's light dies
within me
leaving
hollow
darkened
shell

And there is no one
who can see
I am so lost
in this hell
called life

GROWIN' UP

Frozen
sitting stiff on my father's lap
sharp blade of ice
slicing down spine

Not lying across his legs
like usual
waiting for the blows to fall

Instead
his hard callused hands slide
over the front of my blouse
down across my thighs
around to squeeze my butt

Well, well now girlie
You're growin up right fine
Gonna have that big ole Farroll ass
but ya got some nice little tits coming in
so the boys won't likely mind

Wild panic jolts through me
thrashing madly
I tear myself from his clutching hands
crash out the front door
run

CRYSTAL SHARDS

Specters of the living dead
waft about my bed
and the terror in the nighttime
fills my heart
with dread

Every soul is shrouded
in the darkness of the tomb
and crystal shards of silence
carpet every room

Each misstep met
with searing pain
each scream
with cold disdain

There is no path
to safety
no waking to the light
what is left
is dying

My Soul
at long last
taking
flight

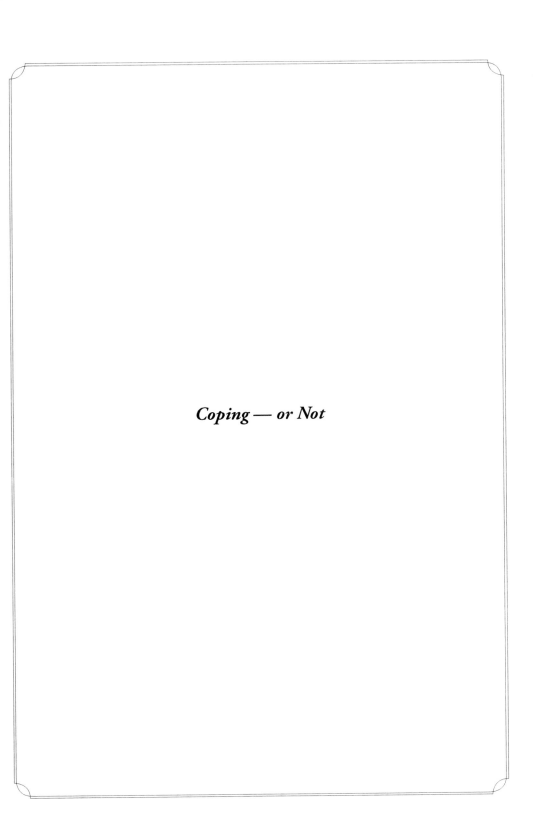

Coping — or Not

SNAPSHOTS

Flash!
Sidelined at recess
watching children play
knowing I am different
they have no idea
what life is really
all about

Flash! Flash!
Sitting in class
staring out through dirty
window panes
teacher's voice
a distant bee-droning
searching for answers
in a clouded sky

Why is he doing this
What will happen
when I get home

Flash! Flash! Flash!
Family picnic
broken glass
screams silenced
bloody prints
on beach blanket

Now look what
you've gone and done
Stupid girl

Flash! Flash!
Flash! Flash!
Near misses
desperate escapes
terror building
knowing the day is coming
when he won't let me go

Flash! Flash!
Flash! Flash! Flash!
dark night
cold curb
headlights approaching
building courage
to jump in front of them
but I never can

Sammie Farroll
Mrs. Schweigert
English

The Long Sleep

Turtle knows the Long Dry is coming. Every day, Hot shines down through pond's water and heats it.

Every day Hot drinks deeper of pond and there is little room to move. Food plants shrivel and die.

At last, Hot beats down on shell and she feels her fragile, flesh body shrink away from its burning touch. Turtle knows it is time to go to the Deep Dark. Slowly, she crawls over crusted pond bottom, reaches its edge and begins to climb its steep sides.

Nearing top, front claws slip free and heavy shell tilts her back over the deep abyss of pond crater. Turtle snaps out long neck and mouth clamps desperately onto root of tree. Strong back legs scramble for purchase and aching neck strains to pull her back, tight against cliff face. Turtle knows to fall onto back is to die. Shivering with fear, Turtle continues her climb.

Gaining cliff's edge at last, she heaves herself out onto the Big Dry. For a moment, she lies there; gulping in great draughts of waterless air and squinting into the harsh glare of Big Bright. With no cool, soothing balm of water through which to see, her eyes ache with the still sharpness of things around her.

Turtle feels the heavy weight of Big Dry lying across her back like a fallen rock, but she pushes her tired body up from the burning hardness of the Big Dry and begins dragging herself to safety. She knows death's shadow can swoop down on her from above or come thundering from the brush, snatching her up and crushing her in snapping jaws.

Heart filled with rushing fear, but body held to a slow crawl, her sharp-clawed feet dig in, drag her forward; dig in, drag her forward, dig in, drag her forward, throughout the eternal day.

Until, at long last, Turtle feels cool shade sliding over her and a merciful softening of Big Bright on her aching eyes. She smells delicious scent of dying leaf and thriving moss and knows she has reached the protective arms of Tree's giant roots; wooden guards that shield her from sight.

Turtle digs wearily into the cool, damp darkness of earth, at last sliding gratefully down into its moist shelter. With waning strength, she pulls the loose dirt over her back and begins to calm. Heart slowing to barely beating, lungs stilled to barely breathing, Turtle slips gratefully into the Long Sleep.

The Long Sleep received 3rd place in the California Writer's Club, Sacramento Branch, Short Story Contest 2012 and Honorable Mention in the Mary Kennedy Eastham Flash Fiction Award, 2011.

REBELLION

Blows of belt
raining down
on welted back

I stand
silent
hidden
deep inside

Smile
Rebellion

BREAKING BACK

Step on a crack
break your mother's back
Step on a space
break your father's face

Carefully
I draw the squares
so the sidewalk joints
fall right in the middle
of each hopscotch box

Chanting
the magic spell
hopefully

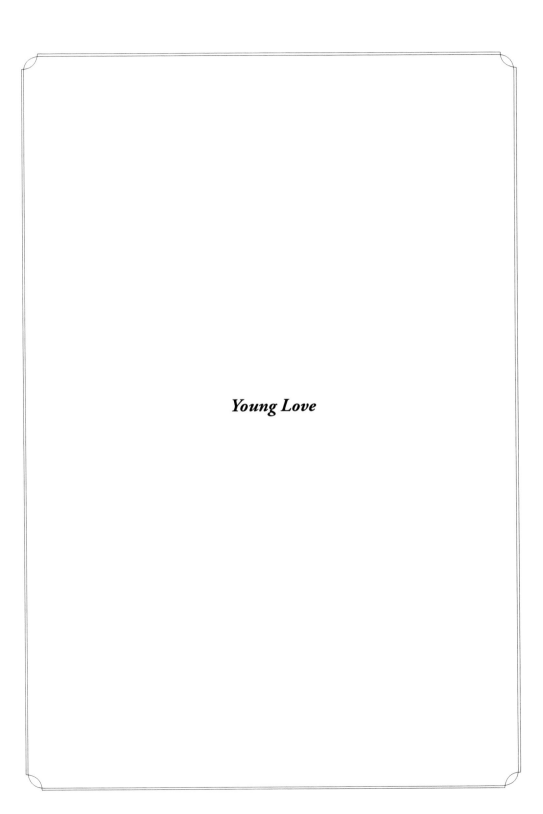

Young Love

LOVE SCORES A RINGER

-i-
Junior high
summer camp
last off the bus
blue-eyed boy calls out

> *Hey, you*
> *come toss some horseshoes*
> *with us*

Shocked
I look around
but no one else
to be found
I shuffle over
eyes cast down
not believing
he wants
me

-ii-

Oh, my God
I never thought
I would be dating

Parents driving
we go skating
to the movies
to the park
we hold hands
in the dark

Warm caresses
soft kisses
head swims
heart sings
we exchange
class rings

SHATTERED

Summer's end
phone rings
his once warm voice
winter cold

Can't see ya no more
my mother says
I ain't got
no choice

Inside
something shatters
razor shards
slicing heart

I feel it tear
I feel it bleed
know I have lost everything
I need

Breath stolen
can't speak
room darkens
stars burst
somehow sitting
on the floor

Aching chest
sucks burning air
into screaming lungs
throat forces broken words
through racking sobs

God No
Please Jerry
let me see you
Just once more

Sullenly
he agrees
picks me up
thin lips
stone face

I am stunned
breathless
shocked
by how quickly
love can disappear
without a trace

Homecoming game
I am benched
between two guards
observing my last request
before execution

Jerry's mother
on one side
closed face
open disdain

He
on the other
eyes cold
back stiff with rejection
right there next to me
but oh so far away

I
Don't
Exist
At
All

With every hit and run
I measure my misery
wondering what foul
what error
what possible sin
did I commit
to drive him so far away
knowing
I'm a loser
even if we win

Time runs out
as it always does
everyone else
jumps and shouts
I sit still
and mute
why pretend
for me I know it's just
The End

Game over for me
always the one
no one will ever
stand up for
or defend

But I can't just let him go
gotta try and make him
stay
and I think I know
the way

Grab his hand
say
I'm sick
take me back
to your place
quick

Burst through door
run into his room
whirl around

Rip open blouse
yellow butterfly buttons
fly free
I
scream

Is this it then, Jerry?
What you really want
All the rest
just a lie

But only shock
not lust
lies in his dark blue eyes

Vision blurs
bones melt
in my heart
I know
the truth

I'm not even
good enough
for this

Face red
Jerry quickly wraps me
in his jacket
like road kill lying in his way
throws me in his car
drives me home
puts me out
at the curb

Staggering inside
I fall into bed
lie there
shattered

Wishing
I
were
dead

HIDING IN OPEN SIGHT

Furnace day outside
so I am holed up
in my only somewhat cooler than
outside
bedroom

Sitting up in bed
shorts-clad
halter topped
reading
my favorite form
of escape

Living in other worlds
where princes rescue
maidens in distress
where dragons are slain
and put to rest

Safe in knowing
my dragon sleeps
within his cave
snoring
smoke and flame

But, no
I am wrong
for he has risen
stalked
stealth-like
down the hall
slipped through
my open door

While I wasn't looking
while I was hiding out
in fairyland

Daddy stands there
at the foot of my bed
face flushed
pale hairy chest
white jockey shorts
with arousal branching out
like the thick limb
of an old oak tree
pointing
right at me

His coal-colored eyes
glassy
gravel voice tight

Hey, girlie
time I showed ya
where babies cum from
reaching down
for his teaching tool

But that small
movement
breaks me from
his swaying cobra
trance

I leap from bed
bolt through door
race to baby sister's room
grab her up and flee
to the backyard

Where we hide now
in open sight
waiting
for Mother Ogre
to come home

Watching
the back door
wondering
which monster
will come through it
first

A WILD, WILD FURIE

A long dark time
of dying
slowly
from the inside
out

Learning there comes
a time of turning
a point when heartbreak
can be no longer borne
When all the tears have run dry
and I discover
It takes more than will alone
to die

Heavy ebony anger
rises up
pushes back
becomes

Wild, Wild Furie
riding a Horse of Hate
throwing back its hydra head and raging
against the lies of fairytales

Prince Charming
coming to the rescue
the safety of Never, Never Land
the promise of
Happily-Ever-After

Parents
don't always love you
homes are not always safe

Innocent little girls fall down
deep, deep holes
landing on giant beds
in miniature palaces
where an Evil Queen
rips away the covers
and yells
Off With Their Heads

And the worm that turns
is a hashish-smoking caterpillar
that transforms and flies away
leaving you behind
to seek a way out
you cannot find

I stand
in the darkness
of the night
and scream
silently

No More, No More
You've pushed me
way too far
No more crying
No more dying
No more trying
to make you love me

THIS IS WAR

Sex — the Good, the Bad & the Ugly

THE BAD ONE

Sweet sixteen
and never been kissed
I laugh bitterly
at the song's silly words

I've been lucky so far
But I know I'll be damned lucky
if he hasn't raped me
long before then

I am the Bad One now
failing grades
always in trouble
rageful

Got caught
stealing a BB gun
for a boy
I hardly knew

Store lets me go
and I flee into the night
rather than go home
to die by my father's hand

But the damn cops pick me up
and take me there anyway
the rest
is lost
to memory

And my body is aflame
insatiably driving me to feed
the ravenous hunger
gnawing there
between my legs
a screaming emptiness
impossible to fill

Disgusted mother assaults me
with the evidence of my efforts

Yells
I yell back
exchange of blows
broken nose

I am the Bad One now
completely out of hand
Bad
for a reason
my mother refuses
to understand

BITTER VICTORY

The time is coming
when he won't let me go
a time when there will finally be
no escaping
no getting past
no place left to run

But I'll be dammed
if he will be
the first!

I invite a blue-eyed boy
to the prom
where
we shuffle
awkwardly around
the huge gym floor

Until my father's stolen booze
has set a sweet fire flowing
through my veins
and I am floating
above the rest

I drag Trey to his car
drive into the dark
we're soon having
Back Seat Sex

After
he lies in stunned surprise
I
in bitter victory

Sammie Farroll
Mrs. Walker
English

A Little Death

Long, jointed body stretches out, pulls in, stretches out, pulls in. Strong legs fine as spider-web rise and fall in undulating waves, like oars sailing me over an ocean of dark green grass.

Fresh breath of day waking whispers over fine hairs of back and cools me. Delicious taste of morning dew fills mouth and I breathe deeply of lush forest floor- life borning, growing, olding, dying, falling, feeding earth again. All ever changing, rearranging, ending, rebeginning all throughout the endless ages.

Sun follows moon. I become heavy and slow, no care to eat. Sleep takes me more and more while my insides turn and twist. I am drawn to Mother Tree. In her shelter I will rest. Inch my way up, a forever time. Crawl under branch and anchor myself to hang there, like a dark leaf - safe at last from beak and claw.

Skin slowly shrinks and peels away. Senses dull and world darkens though it is day. Thoughts recede and I die.

Faint light filters through shrunken cloth of my old body and a hunger for life awakens me. Strong feet pierce soft restraint and I tear my way to freedom. Crawling out onto broad branch I rest, letting warmth of sun caress and dry me. Sweet smell of flower calls – I spread my wings and fly.

SOARING

I am soaring
through a liquid
moon-filled night

Gliding along under
the million trillion
brilliant stars
of the Milky Way

Flying higher
than Peter Pan
ever could

Head thrown back
arms flung wide
sharing my joy
with the world

Steep climb behind me
I am coasting
knowing it's all downhill
from here to His house

My quiet rebellion
is working I think
Father forbid us
from riding to school together
but we did it anyway

Until that awful day when
Trey came to the bus stop to get me
and dad came screeching up to block him in
face swollen and red with anger
grabbed my arm and drug me
kicking and screaming
back to his car and threw me in
while Trey and my friends
just stood there in silent shock
helpless to save me

So now instead
I lie wide-eyed in bed
until I'm sure the Dragon
and Ogre are both asleep
then sneak quietly out of the house
tiptoe my bike silently to the street
jump on and launch myself
into my nightly pilgrimage to Him

Speeding across town
my heart racing
faster than my bike's wheels

Finally arriving to tap softly
on his unlocked window
slip through and fall into
his eager embrace

I relish the rushed removal
of innocence in the form of clothes
marvel at the feel of touching
and being touched
the velvety sensation of skin on skin
the incredible sense of safety I have
lying in his arms

We tickle and tease
wrestle and roll around
stifling our laughter
so his parents won't hear

Then at last
a few brief moments
of enthusiastic calisthenics
a feeling like he's peeing inside me
he slumps down
falls asleep

I lie there and watch him breathe
for the longest time
telling myself
that it doesn't really matter
if he pees inside of me
or that the sex isn't like
what's in my father's books

No pounding passion
no piercing screams of ecstasy
no hour long orgasms

As I ride into the night
I know
nothing else really matters
now
that
I
am
loved

BROKEN SILENCE

Warm butt on cool tile
tanned legs dangling
over the edge of the school pool
toes dipping into
crystal clear coldness
refreshing
on an already hot July day

I sit and watch Trey
Stroke, stroke, stroke
from one end to the other
his strong hard body
gliding through the liquid blue
like a beautiful harbor seal
a rhythm I remember so well
from just the night before

Taking swimming lessons
seemed like a good way
to be together in the mornings
or at least we thought so
at the time

But I can only sit and watch
as my stomach roils just like
the pool's surface
as Trey cuts through it

Must have been something I ate
Maybe that chili dog yesterday
or the flu that's been going round school

Definitely the flu
I decide
after four awful days
of losing my breakfast
every morning on the bus

Reluctantly
I tell my mother
fully expecting her to tell me
to get over it
but she looks at me oddly
and silently walks away

The next morning
as I lie there in bed
too sick now
to even go to the pool
she opens my bedroom door
closes it behind her

Uh oh
Is she going to yell at me
for being sick
or bug me again about
those suspicious stains
on my underwear

But face twisted with disgust
she says instead
I've made an appointment with the family doctor
but, before I take you in
and have to face him
I wanna know
is there any chance
you could be pregnant

A bright flash of knowing
pierces my brain
a broken dam's worth
of rage roaring out
steel muzzle of silence broken

Yes
I growl through gritted teeth
But I don't wanna hear
nothin out of you
cause Dad's been messin with me
for years

And for the first time in my life
my mother stands speechless
turns slowly
opens my door
walks out
closing it
quietly
behind her

JUST AS WELL

Trey and I sit stiff
in the back seat
of the family car

Heading for another county
where we can get married
bein' under sixteen and all

So much for high school
I think
just as well
I wasn't doing so good there
anyway
too stupid

And I hated trying to cover it up
asked my father for a note
saying I didn't have to try
and speak Spanish
in front of the whole class
couldn't bear the humiliation
I get enough of that at home

Liked using his power
on the one hand
felt awful
on the other

So much for home
I think
as it recedes into my past

But
just
as
well

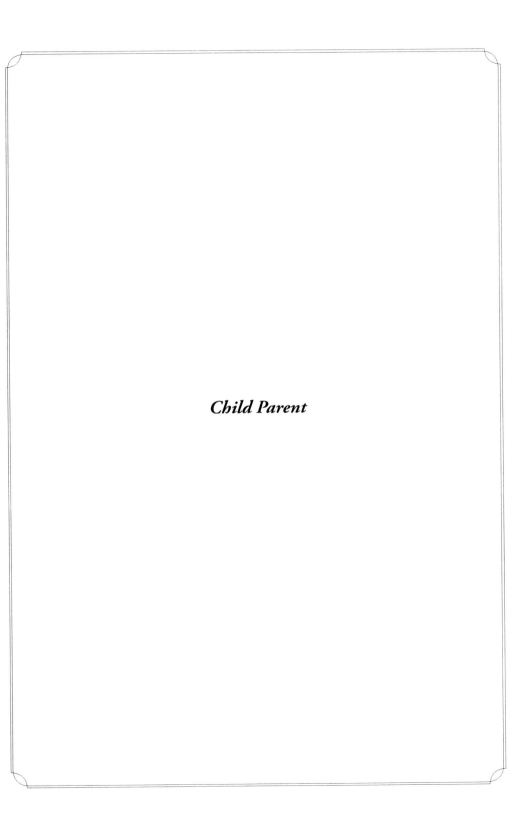

Child Parent

SOLITARY CONFINEMENT

After getting hitched
Trey and I move across town
where he can work
in his step-father's cleaners
and I can stay home
and incubate

Six long months
of Solitary Confinement
though terribly bored
I relish the complete safety
of my aloneness

But am horrified
at how my belly grows
to bursting size
a summer melon
left too long
in the field

My reflection
a House of Mirrors version
of my real body

Me
but somehow
not

But at least
as I've come to term
I have learned
the important difference
between pee and sperm

Finally understand
that last lesson
Daddy tried to teach
me and thank God
this baby
isn't his

GAME TIME

Nine and a half months
though huge
worn thin

Unsure if we're into overtime
or it's just faulty score keeping
on my part
can't wait to get this kid
out of me
so tired of being pummeled
by its indoor football games

Late night
babysitting
at the in-laws house
while they're out
dancing and boozing
bunch of wild savages
them and their little hellions

Trey comes over after work
we sit at the kitchen table
drinking
but my gut begins to twist
like a wet towel being wrung dry
    just for a minute
        then again
        and again

       Hey, Trey
       I think it's
       game time

    We race away
    into the night
to score a little hellion touchdown
    of our own

LIGHT BLUE EYES

Nurses take one look at me
and decide I'm too young
for this X-rated event
give me a shot and
I am gone

Wake up groggy
mother sitting silent
next to the bed

Hey, mom
I think my water broke
that baby should be here
any time now

You've already had it
she says quietly

Wake up groggy
in-laws standing
at the foot of the bed
at least this time I remember
I've had the baby

Have they put her in
the refrigerator yet

Then at last
there's a tiny baby on my chest
miniature toes and fingers
curly blond hair
and yes
light blue eyes

TWO CHILDREN AND A CHILD

Miniature fingers
clinging to mine
big blue eyes
that sparkle and shine
my own personal little
"bundle of joy"

But definitely not
a toy
needs all of my attention
all of the time
whimpers and cries
through night and day
no matter what anyone tries
cannot seem to find her way
to sleep

Colicky baby will hardly eat
and when she does
just can't seem to keep
it down

Projectile vomiting
the doctor names it
and I have to laugh

Yep, it's an inborn skill I'm told
and my grandpappy claims it

Why, I'll always remember
him and his cronies rockin'
out on the front porch
hot breath of summer
singeing the dry air
like a torch

Spittin' tobaccie
over the weathered wooden rail
just to see how far away
it would sail

Dark brown dashes
left like Morse code
upon the hard parched earth
private messages
to each other
of brotherhood's worth

They lay in wait
for the winter rain
to wash their silent secrets
down the drain

The doc and I
have a good laugh
and think it's a hoot
that this little girl
could probably outshoot
all of them by half

But baby's daddy
doesn't think it's funny at all
acts like it's Vesuvius erupting
and runs the other way
comes down with
an acute case of B. F. A.
Bodily Fluid Avoidance

Refuses
to hold her
hear her
feed her

Give her anything
she really needs
to thrive
shoves her off on me
to keep alive

I
am alone
with this problem
called
life

DARK SHADOW

Four months into
solo duty
my loving coos
shift to shouts
I become prone
to impatience
and lashing out

Finally I snap
from lack of sleep
and her incessant crying
throw her on the bed
but with a bounce
soft head
hits hard edge

Screams
blood
fear
shame

A lifelong scar
bearing my name
forever a reminder
of just how far
I can go
what I can be

I feel the dark shadow
    of my father
      falling
        over
         me

DISHONORABLE DISCHARGE

Afraid
of the feral animal
that is my anger

Terrified
it might escape its cage
and grow
into my father's deadly rage
I turn and flee

I desert the front lines
of motherhood
find just cause
for a dishonorable discharge
become a turncoat
for the other side

Start working
for the evil in-laws
in a place where they make
 everything clean
 and I can't hear
 my baby's cries
 over the soothing roar
of a laundry machine

As my life begins
to rearrange
I am amazed to discover
I can actually learn
to make change
for others
maybe I'm not such a
stupid girl
after all

Except of course
when it comes to my own
daughter
who has shown me that
I'm a lousy mother

Must take after my own
I think
and shudder
at such a horrible
thought

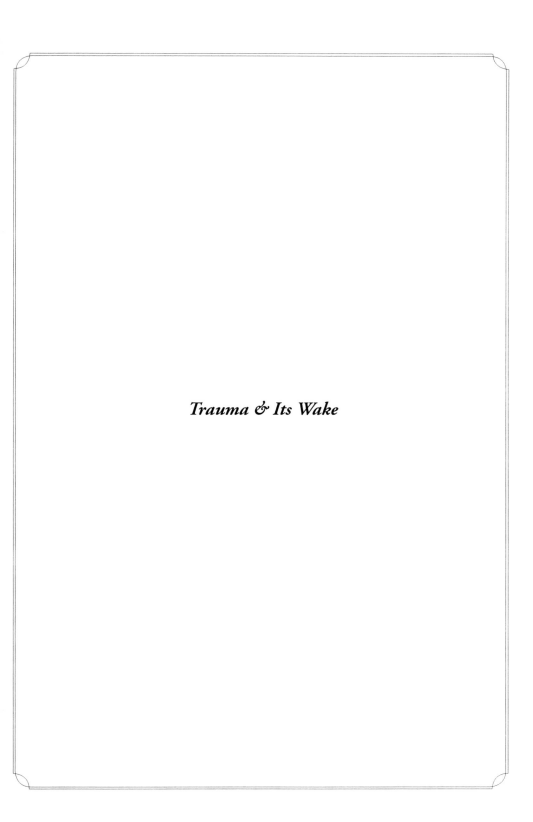

Trauma & Its Wake

REGRET

Two years go by
in a flash
with me enjoying work
more and more
Trey
less and less

"Rode hard
and put away wet"
he stumbles home to crash
his words short
manner curt

Too tired
to give me much
an invisible daughter
he will not touch

His sad blue eyes
filled with nothing
but
regret

SEVEN COME ELEVEN

Seven-eleven man
looks me up
and down
begins to flirt
seems to think I'm cute

High on the power
and the lure of the unknown
I slip off my wedding band
follow him home

Noon time nookie
anything goes
wild bronco
breaking in
racing hands
bouncing bed
flying clothes
ages old
original sin

Far too soon
he's done and sleeps
while I lie there
amid tumbled sheets
    reeking of
        Brut
      sweat
       sex

Staring up blankly
at the rain-stained ceiling
I mourn
the unfulfilled promise
of porn

No ecstasy of infidelity
just one more thing
I've gone and done
that justifies
my mother's scorn

But at least I tried
and having his attention
is better than having
none

After all
everyone knows
that life is full of lies
and I've grown used to
keeping hidden
the forbidden

EMPTY HOUSE

Already one foot out
the door
Trey helps me leave
with a final shove
not of me
but the one I bore
all that remains
of our lost love

Weekend warrior
football fan
sits with feet up
on the TV stand
beer in one
nuts
in the other
hand

Thrilled to see him
when she wakes
our daughter
is a running back
fiercely locked
upon her goal
racing towards
her father
eager to leap
into the end zone
of his heart

But an angry frown
and one stiff arm
is all it takes
to knock her down
tear her fragile soul
apart

White hot rage
burns through
what little bond
with spouse
is left

Trey comes home
the next night
to an empty
house

ALONE

Though filled with fear
I scurry back home again
to the only thin semblance
of safety
I have ever known

Lie awake at night
clutching my daughter
and listening
for the dreaded fall
of footsteps
in the hall

As quickly as I can
I find a place and move
Just a dump
but at least
my own

But am overwhelmed
by the terror
of being
alone

Sliding down
toward insane
my days
become a blur of work
my nights
I drown in drink

So I don't have to feel
the pain
So I don't have to
think

Bad Seed

STONES

I walk the silent
hallowed halls
of my old high-school
and realize
I am so lost

Standing before
glass cases
still hanging
on the old brick walls
I recognize
familiar faces

And even though
so long ago
I still can see
scornful judgment
in their eyes

Still hear
a haunting echo of
snickers
stifled laughs
whispers

There goes that stupid
little slut
who screwed around
and got knocked up

Memories
heavy stones
of self-blame
added to the mountain of
my shame

Though my pregnancy
an unplanned rescue
from my plight
would anything
I could ever do
throw off its weight
or make up for
its heavy cost

SUPERNOVA

Hey there missy
you look lost
Can I help you find
where you're going

Snapped from silent reverie
I whirl around to see
a handsome janitor
who wasn't there before
slipped up on me
without my knowing

His light blue eyes
sweep sensuously over me
just like the broom he sweeps
across the floor

Then he stops and stands
strong brown hands slowly stroking
thick hard wood of handle
held in front of him

His hot gaze tracing
a trail of fire
across my body
my face ablaze
with heat

I...I... can't seem to find
the...the... room
where I sign... sign... up
for...for... the typing class
I stutter
when finally able
to speak

He sets his broom aside
ambles over and takes my arm
like he owns it

Well now, little lady
I'd be more than happy
to take you
just come
along with me

When I'm done
we go for a coke
then I take him
home

Where I am
blown apart
by passion
that has no boundaries
no rules
no walls

Whatever
small town modesty
was left in me
he strips away
and it falls
to dust

Obliterated by
irrepressible
ceaseless
pile-driving
pounding
thrusting
diamond head
drill bit
sounding
deep well

Roaring
fills my ears
thoughts lose meaning
senses reeling
vaguely hearing
distant screaming

I
become
only
feeling

HOLE IN THE WALL

Hard sex
sound sleep

CRASH!

Foot not yet to floor
Trey silhouetted
in the bedroom door
long rifle barrel aimed
like an accusing steel finger
right at our bed

Up against the wall
Asshole

Tousled hair
tangled sheets
Jerry struggles
to free himself
and finally stands
shivering
in the hot room
trying
to cover his impressive cock
with too-short hands

I lie mute
not believing for a moment
Trey will shoot
and perversely hoping
he will take in the scope
of his own shortcomings

Where's your
fucking license
Trey snaps

But Jerry
frozen in place
stares helplessly
at the traitorous wallet
lying just out of reach
on the dresser

BANG!

Shot deafening
in the small room
acrid smell of gun powder
sharp in the heavy air

My head whips back
from Trey to Jerry
        but he is
        not dead
          short
          not tall

He stands staring
at a small black hole
in the wall
just above his head

Trey shouts
Jerry leaps
grabs his wallet
throws it down
at my husband's feet

Who picks it up
and turns towards
the baby's crib

Jumping to block his way
I am slammed into the dresser
ribs cracked
I slump breathless to the floor
stunned by the pain of knowing
I have only myself
to blame

Babe in arms
Trey leaves
Jerry turns tail
and flees

Afraid Trey might return
I call my father to the rescue
he arrives carrying his own gun
sleeps in front of the busted door

I lie awake all night
eyes riveted
to the ominous
black portal of hell
that is my bedroom door
praying to God
he doesn't do
anything more

UNFIT

Trey holds our baby
hostage
and cuts a deal
no child support
or a custody fight

Since adultery
equals unfit
in this state
I give in

Take back my baby
take off my ring
count my blessings
knowing that
once again

Sex
has almost cost me
everything

Drugs, Sex & Rock n Roll

PURPLE HAZE [1]

Jerry takes me
heart and soul
fills my days with
Sex
Drugs
Rock 'n roll

Puff the Magic Dragon [2]
takes me
without a sound
deep into a
Purple Haze

T
   i
      m
        e
S
  l
    o
      w
       s
D
  o
    w
      n

Thoughts fly away

Acid potion
candles flicker
with no motion
no night
no day

Floating
on a rainbow
cloud
casting off
my shadow
shroud

Burning incense
smells
sounds
touch
turning intense

No yesterday
no tomorrow
no more pain
no more sorrow

No more
Helter Skelter [3]
deep inside
I find release
a place to shelter
a place to hide

    In complete
      inner
      peace

MAD MAD WORLD [4]

Right outside
the magic door remains a
Mad Mad World
that never pauses

Skies full of flying witches
ever chasing after lost causes
want to throw those
nuclear switches

Civil Rights marches
across the land
Panthers stalking
Klu Klux Klan
with their torches

Feminist
and
Labor pains
movements
giving birth to change

Un-united Nations
losing patience
shoe pounding
screaming loud
Tricky Dicktator
wants to see
that mushroom cloud

Vietnam soldiers
Dying
Blue Monkeys
Flying
Napalm skies
Crying
Vets live to become
dead junkies

Shooting star
in my bed
open window
cold draft
we get wed
run shouting
from the altar
Hell no
he won't go
to war

MISSING IN ACTION

But on the home front
something slips
something slides
somehow peace
rolls over
and dies

He's agitated
never sleeps
mood erratic
swells and peaks
anger waking
cresting rage
finally breaking
from its cage

Things get busted
things explode
he packs his car
with all he owns
squealing tires
lost traction
Gone Missing
In Action

Endless tears
heart rusted
doctor phones
Jerry's in Virginia
some disease
too many unknowns

*Can you come and get him
please*

From here to there
things go south
mumbling zombies
walk the halls
small white room with
padded walls

Designer wear
long-sleeved jacket
tied in back
blank stare
jaw slack
drooling mouth

But this time not
hallucinogenic
rather something weird called
schizophrenic

BACK INTO THE VOID

Mad Hatter
quiet and still
just won't take that
small orange pill
reality starts
to tatter

Tailspin
going down
thinks both the cops
and KKK
want to take him in
wants to hightail it out of
town

But by now I know
I can't take my child
and go
anywhere with him
when he's so lost
in outer space
living on planet paranoid
so I stand and watch him
drive away

Hearing in my heart
Gabriel's horn a'calling
know that somewhere
deep inside
something dear
has died
cause I can feel myself
falling

Back
into
the
Void

GROUND ZERO

My soul
ground zero
utter devastation
bottomless crater
black hole
sucking in all light

Tear ducts broken
no off valve
monsoon season
drowning me in sorrow

I am
Walking Wounded
can't eat
sleep
breathe
think
work

Assaulted on all sides
by painful reminders
of what I've lost
what I let
walk away
I lie curled in
fetal position
my bed
his scent

Finally fleeing
a deadly firestorm
of burning memories
I give up
all I own

Second hand furniture
returned to the first
or given to a third
down to six boxes
and one small child
I board a Greyhound
speeding east
at a snail's pace

ARRESTED DEVELOPMENT

In North Carolina
I marvel
at my cousin's youth

Fresh out of high school
still living at home with mommy
church on Sunday's

I wear
a shag haircut
crop top
paisley print hip-huggers
two marriage's
under my belt
hemp sandals
and a two-year old
on my hip

Though the same age
 I feel old

Intent on moving my cousin
into the sixty's
I rent a small house
with no heat
and take her there

Try to teach her to loosen up
smoke dope
have no-strings-sex with strangers
but find that she's hopelessly Christian

I however
indulge in both
though numb
feeling somehow compelled
to go through the motions

Until one day
I get the news
Jerry's back in Texas
ranting
resisting arrest
thrown in jail

I know
he went back for me
am sure a song on the radio
My Baby Wrote Me a Letter[5]
is a cosmic message
from him
to me
to come back

I
six boxes
baby and bus
crawl back to Texas
as fast as we can

JUNKIE

Back to my girlfriend's
warm embraces
back to all
the old familiar faces

Drinking
drugging
dancing
screwing passing for
romancing

Nobody eats
nobody sleeps
we're all just passing time
living in sin

Oh boy
Happy Days
are Here Again

But I am walking
the dark night streets
searching for a Jerry
who's gone missing
no longer in jail
and nobody's talking

Is he alive or dead
off his meds
off his head

Gone to heaven
gone to hell
no one will say
no one will tell
but everyone knows
he's probably wherever it is
that craziness goes

But it doesn't really matter
since I can't climb out
of this bottomless hole I've dug

Even if he is mad as a hatter
I'm still a junkie
and he's still
my
drug

Last Straw, First Love

SETTLE IN

I settle in to wait
go back to work
for the ex in-laws
but far away from their son
The Jerk

I'm in a store right down town
located conveniently close
to a bar
no going home first
to see the kid
why think of the cost of gas
it's just way too far

So I simply arrange
for mother to take care
of her instead

It's about time
she was there for someone
for a change
before she's dead

NASTY WEATHER

Thank God it's Friday
head uptown
hit the bars
party down

Happy hour
sad heart
grief still tearing me
apart

I sit desperately trying
to drown sorrow
so there is no yesterday
or tomorrow

Friends bring over
some lonely dude
I could care less
but can't be rude

Suddenly
there's a plan
go to my friend's place
take this man

We're hardly in
before they're out
leave the living room
lock the bedroom door
left me alone to cope
with this idiot
The Boar

We smoke more dope
then he insists
we do the nasty
on the floor

For once
I'm having none
yet he persists
says I'll be happy
when he's done

Saturday night wrestling
main event
decides to take me
without consent

He's strong
but I'm stronger
noise gets louder
as it goes on longer

I start to worry
I'll be a bother
disturb my friends
if this goes farther

So I take
the fight outside
play tag in the courtyard
circle the pool
torn dress
what a fool

Why's he making
such a fuss
paw the ground
roar and cuss

Idiot's going to wake up
the whole complex
Come on guy
it's only sex

Ok you creep
let's get a room
I know it'll be over soon
and sure enough
two seconds later
he's sound asleep

Get up
pin my dress
grab a bus
no harm, no foul
more or less

Hot forehead
icy pane
soul frozen solid
neither alive nor dead

Hope fading slowly
out of sight
it's nasty weather
and the
darkest dark
of night

HERE IN ABSENTIA

Empty year to follow
heart dead
soul hollow
my life becomes
an X-rated movie house
with sticky floors
and pimps
at all the doors

I a silent actor
flickering across
a worn thin screen
passive participant
in each short scene

Scene 1- LAY LAWYER

I hire a lawyer
to divorce Jerry
in absentia

Driving back from court
he turns to me and smiles
I don't suppose
it'll take you long
to get a new man
with breasts like those

I don't know what to say
wonder
if he's hitting me up
for a bonus lay

Scene 2- JUST DESSERTS

Boss invites me out to lunch
begins to flirt
slides his hand
far up my skirt
realize
I'm for dessert

Only fools believe
men play
by the rules

Scene 3- AUTO EROTIC

Brother-in-law
driving me somewhere
or another

You sure got all the breasts
in this family
he declares as he reaches over
with a firm grasp to measure
the objects
of his pleasure

Scene 4- MILKMAN RINGS TWICE

I don't think your sister's really mine
my father shares
in a self-pitying whine

Oh come on dad
she looks just like you
I reply
even though I know
it's just not true

It would serve him right
I think
if the man that really delivered
also brought the milk we
drink

Scene 5- DYING DAY

Dad drives me over
in his loaded truck
the only way to move my stuff
even though I know
it's pushing my luck

All done
I declare at last
trying my best
to quickly edge past

Except for this
he growls and grabs me
tries to kiss

Breaking away
racing to his car
wondering
will I be running
'til my dying day

LAST STRAW

That's it
I've had enough
I'm sick and tired of trying
to do it right
to be tough

This is the last straw
as far as I'm concerned
no more reaching out
only to get burned

So Screw You
and all your kin
you don't know jack
about where I've been

It's time I was
finally true
to myself
my life
and

You

HOME

Double dating but all the while
hearing only your laughter
seeing only your smile

Savoring the scent of your perfume
even long after you've left
the room

Aching to touch you
but so afraid
damnation and death
the price to be paid

Sure wreck and ruin
the Christians shout
*Against the Lord's will
what you're doin'*

Inevitable tragedy
in my father's books
faggots burned at the stake
strung up on hooks

But still the longing grows
wonder if she sees it
wonder if she knows

Sleeping over
I watch her breathe
feeling the pain in my heart
only she can relieve

Wishing she was more
than just a friend
wishing I could kiss her
even when
she was the little girl
next door

Lost in my reverie
I don't know when
Alex awakens and sees
I can no longer pretend

Her aqua eyes gazing
deep into mine
we slip into a world
outside of time

Two hearts
at long last beating
to love's steady metronome
at long last feeling
I am finally
home

She strokes my face
sighs my name
and I know that all
will be well
for no hope for heaven
or fear of hell
can continue to restrain

This
our
loving
fall
from
grace

ETERNITY

Does your heart have room
for all I have to give
Does it have an endless place
wherein I could live

If it does then let me move in
for now and evermore
slowly
gently
opening
each and every door

Discovering
how deep
you will let me travel
how high
you will let me go
as I carefully unravel
all there is to know

Having every inch
and all of you
nothing else
could ever do

Loving each other through
the smoothest times
as well as through the rough
Loving through all Eternity
will hardly be
time
enough

Trauma & Rebirth

INTERLUDE

Coin flipping
through thin air

Choice or chance choosing
love
or
despair

My future hanging
on the turn of a dime
will Alex stay with men
or will she be
mine

Hope
once soaring
dashed
promises
once given
trashed

Love poems
ripped apart
fall among the shards
of my shattered heart

For her
just a lovely interlude
tribute
to a childhood shared

For me
my soul flayed open
left lying here
as if she never cared

I watch her go
and know
I stand condemned
to eternal
solitude

DAD DEFEATED

I watch my father fade
into shadow
life draining slowly
from his soul

I see the knowledge grow
the wages of his sins
soon
to be paid

Former strength depleted
head hangs slack
on sunken chest
pride broken
rage defeated

What passed for a heart
is breaking
God's retribution finally
in the making

On the surgeon's table
the sands of time
spill out

My father dies and yet
I wonder if
justice
is truly
mine

FORMAL GRIEF

Family funeral
Formal grief
odd regret warring
with relief

People must think
I'm heartless too
I don't cry
the way they do

All I feel
is deep
emptiness

Alex leaves
Dad dies
I am so tired
of all these lies

HERE BE DRAGONS

Walking away
black rose wreath
a life full of pain
sorrow
grief

His the only mooring
His the only hand
my one and only shoring
in a vast and empty land

I am adrift
lost at sea
so long ago cut loose
from family

Were we once
upon a time
one continent
one heart
somehow shattered
then drifting far apart

Solitary islands
fading into fog
as the inking of our kinship
faded
from ancient slave ships log

Now I float here
becalmed at harbor's gate
though my passage
long since paid
the guarding dragon slain
still
I hesitate

In this dark of day
do I dare
set sail blind
no map to show the way
only an ominous warning
Here be dragons
of an unknown kind

Three times bereft
the Void is calling
no anchor left to stay
my lonely ship from falling
off the sharp edge of the earth

But I know that somewhere
out there
my future's found unfurled

With trembling hand
I cut the dock line
surrender to the fates
pray benign whatever odyssey
awaits

For there is no tacking back
to a life I can no more pretend
has ever served me well

The winds of change are blowing
and I launch myself
not knowing
if what lies at voyage's end
be heaven
or be hell

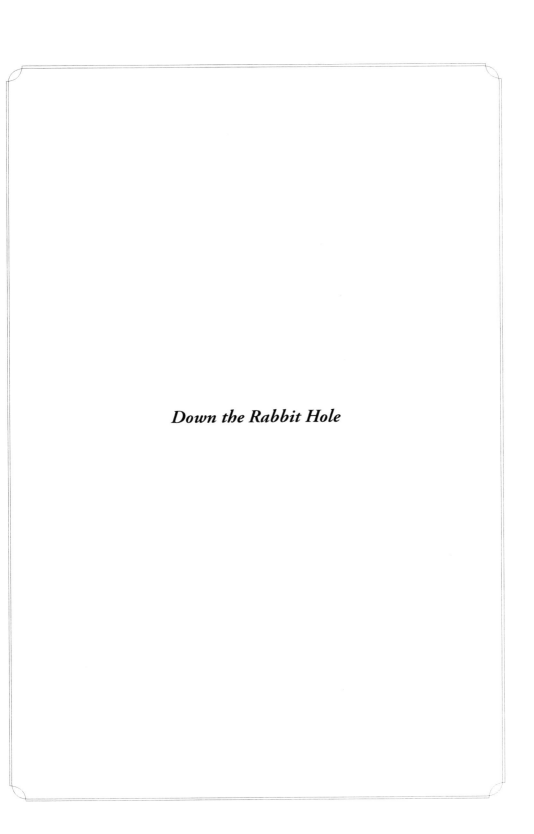

Down the Rabbit Hole

LANDFALL

Circumnavigating
the shaggy shores
of Galveston Island
I make landfall
still staggering
on sea legs
grown accustomed
to imbalance

Skulk black alleyways
ripe as bilge water
desperately seeking
some kindred outlaws
some hidden den of iniquity
pirates' stronghold
Robbers Roost
Hole-in-the-Wall
I can call
home

Collapse at last
in a dingy bar
hoping to quench my thirst
for hopelessness

To my surprise
some patron saint
has led me to
a Joel Gray impersonator
right out of
Cabaret

Who later agrees
to show me where
one goes if one
happens to be
queer

GREEN DOOR [6]

Wrong side of the tracks
shantiest part of shanty town
even cops steering clear
and looking leery

Trench coats with collars up
we walk through a long dark alley
to basement steps
going down

Law defied
you knock three times
on the locked green door
a gruff query and you reply
Dorothy sent us

The yawning maw
of a black pit opens
and I tumble through
freefall plunge onto
the upper floor
of the under world

A Cheshire grin hangs in open space
a disembodied voice welcomes
Hello, homo
Come on in
You've found the right place

I turn to you
with dismay
and whisper
Gee, Quasimodo
I don't think
we're in Kansas
anymore

ENDS UP

Eager eyes stinging
I squint blindly into
a thick blue haze
of fag smoke

    Dank dark cave
  breath held back from
  the sickening smell of
      cigarettes
        booze
          sweat
            puke
            dope
              piss

Juke box bass
a crashing wave of sound
smashing against
the delicate reef
of my ears

Someone
something
passes by clearing
a brief portal of vision
through the dense fog

What
No
this can't possibly be
the right place
why look at that he-man trucker

But a small-framed
sweet faced
swivel-hipped boy
weaves slowly through the tables
and sidles up to him
rubs painted on pants
against a broad
plaid shirt covered shoulder
and asks with silky voice

Should I take you
or your order first Mary
your choice

Large hirsute paw
reaches out to squeeze
the tightly packed seat
of his affections

Well now, little darlin'
why don't you give me
some of those tasty nuts first
and then we'll see what I can
come up with to wash 'em down

My mind madly reshuffles
    outdated records
     antique tapes
ripping off all the old labels

       Fag
      Fairy
      Sissy
     Pansy
     Queer

All those words
so hard and mean
flung like rocks
at small meek boys
like my brother
just to make them cry
just to make them run

And yet I still believed them
still bought the stereotypes
stunned and reeling
I stumble my way
through the dingy dark
to hide as best I can
in the farthest corner
of the farthest booth
my back against the wall

The only female here
my new friend long lost
I sit sipping sweet vermouth
and simply stare
just waiting for the white rabbit
and Mad Hatter to appear

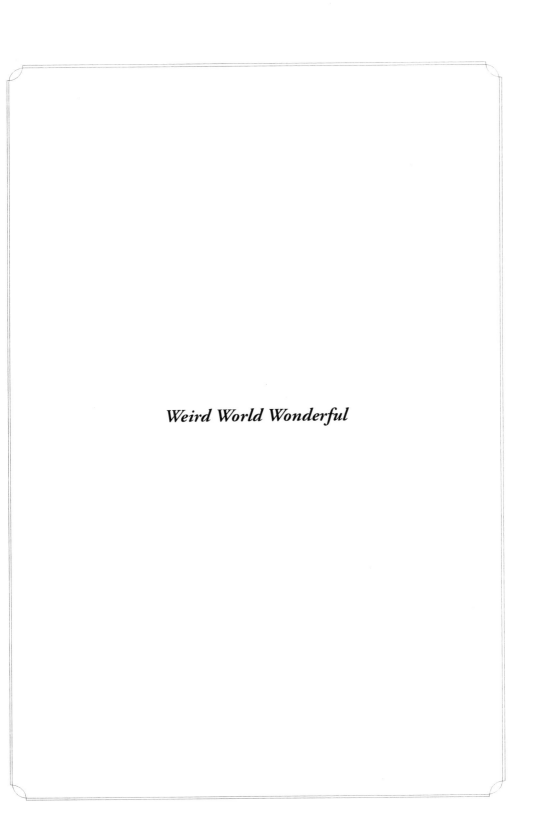

Weird World Wonderful

JUST HUMAN WAYS

From the pulpit
from the porn
I know I am now an
abomination against God
just another faceless object
subject to public ridicule
and private scorn

After all
it's just human nature
it's just human ways

Righteous Right
preach'n hate
give their bless'n
teach those women and faggots
a burning lesson

They never seem to learn
witch hunts never end

Settlers swarming over
Natives' land
give typhoid blankets
to Redskins just trying
to make a stand

Indians are left
with reservations

Chinese building
our east-west way
their lives railroaded
for a dollar a day
finally strike out
for equal pay

Starved into submission
their sunken graves leave
a thousand Chinks
in our walls

Hitler rages
a blazing furnace
United Nations blind
to Jewish purging
until one of their own falls

Death has to be walking
through our door
before we hear
it knocking

Broken Pearl
yet nothing learned
harbor resentments
get Japs interned

So many lives and lands lost
we're still paying
the cost

Ku Klux Klan decline
basic human rights
when Blacks protest in earnest
white sheets leave them hanging
on a line

State against state
brother against brother
we can't get far
because there's nothing
Civil
about war

Hate and prejudice
turn us against
each other

All throughout our history's pages
Jackboots of oppression
smashing down on
freedom's wings

Even as we say
hope springs eternal
and a cracked Liberty Bell
rings

I have to wonder
will there ever be a day
when it sings
for me

LAVENDER DOOR

Long lilac-filled hedges led to the light lavender door of the lesbian bar. The blossoms' sweet scent hanging heavy in the humid night air. A dim yellow light over the entryway softly illuminated the moss-brown flagstones of the path. Though just as anonymous as its male counterpart, this homosexual hide-away was clearly on the Oz side of the rainbow. While the other had skulked sullenly at the back of a long dark alley, this entryway into the underworld lay hidden in plain sight under the guise of a lovely cottage home.

No defiant name upon the door screamed its forbidden nature into the straight-laced Texas streets. No thumping, bass-heavy music pounded its way through smoke covered windows to assault the ears of a sleeping suburban neighborhood. Only the faintly detectable strands of a Viennese waltz wafted gently through delicate glass windowpanes to float lightly over the lush green Bermuda-grass, quickly dissipating into the air like an early morning mist. The only clue to suggest that I was, according to the Christian Right, in the wrong place, was the subtle address etched deeply into a burnished brass plate - 2469.

So I hovered nervously before the lavender door, heart racing like the blurred wings of a hummingbird. Was this really the right place? Was the door locked, like the *Ends Up*, requiring some secret knock and arcane password to gain entry? Or would a simple turn of the knob open the door to my future? Once in, would I be allowed to stay? I was never sure since I lived in a legal limbo land.

Only twenty years old, I was still under the legal age to drink in Texas. But I had been married, not once but twice- an instant ticket to adulthood here. However, I was also twice divorced so not really sure if I'd been demoted back to illegitimacy or not. So, whenever I approached a new bar I was always afraid I'd be carded and rejected at the door. I would stand there watching anxiously as some burly guardian of morality stood shifting his eyes slowly from my still-childish face to the "Mrs." on my driver's license. Debating with himself, I'm sure, the relative risks of being busted by the law if it was a fake ID versus the benefits of reeling an attractive young fish into his club's own private pool.

In fact, whenever possible, I tried to increase my chances of admission by draping myself on the arm of some obviously older man who might, just possibly, be the "Mr." granting me legitimacy. I further hedged my bets by wearing the tightest skirt, highest heels and lowest-cut blouse that I owned, looking up at him seductively with my blue-shadowed, heavily mascaraed eyes and softly purring, "Really, I'm legal, trust me," in my best Mae West voice.

But no male escort would be allowed into this secrete bastion of female deviance. No, here I stood alone, powerless to affect my acceptance or rejection. Not even knowing if I'd like what I found if I did get in. After all, I'd already been conned by the stories in my father's porn books twice now- once about how great sex with men was (except for Jerry, of course) and again about the "feyness" of homosexual men. What would real lezzie's look like- the luscious women of *The Third Sex* or the sadistic she-males of *Satan's Daughters*?

Yet, I knew it didn't really matter. I had to figure out my feelings once and for all. Fortified by the three drinks and a joint I'd already had, I took a ragged breath, reached out and turned the cold brass doorknob.

ROCKY PASSAGE

Slipping quickly through the door
I keep my eyes down
rely on magical thinking
They won't see me
if I don't see them

Sense my way
to the bar
a bee honing in
on honey

Sliding silently onto a stool
I try to be invisible enough
not to get noticed
but seeable enough to get the drink
so desperately needed

Hi there honey
haven't seen you in here before
a soft voice says
as small disembodied hand
slips into my narrowed field of vision
swiping a damp rag over the hopelessly stained
and pitted countertop

My name's Rocky
what's yours
the voice asks
my still-bowed head

With fear locking throat
my right hand clasped desperately
around a small black purse
I can only reach out clumsily with my left hand
for an awkward handshake
and stutter out my name

Finally I look up fearfully
to find a warm and sympathetic gaze
filled to the brim with knowing

It's ok kid
I hear her say
You're safe here with me
and I feel a lifetime's worth
of loneliness
slowly melt
away

LESBIAN LAND

Four straight shots
of courage later
I can finally lift my head
turn and see my
Brave New World

Shadowy figures
stand sit wander about
a dark and smoky room

Short slicked-back hair
plaid-shirted pool players
swaggering around
green felt-topped tables
packs of fags held tight against
muscular biceps
by rolled up sleeves

I stare
confused and disbelieving
but yes
as shirts fall flat
against covered chests
I can barely discern
the hidden mounds
of a woman's breasts

And in my own I feel
the disappointed sinking of hope
as it slides down into
despair
Why in the world
I ask myself
would I want a female version
of a man

But as my eyes continue straining
to pierce the thick blue smoke
I am relieved at last to see
several bouffant hairdo's raising
high above the backs of
dark red leather booths

Thank God
I blaspheme
at least there are some
Real women here

SHARK BAIT

Weeks pass
butt glued to barstool
while Rocky introduces me
to each new woman
who sidles up
to get a drink
and a quick look-see
at the new bee

Finally I am able
to pry myself away
from the safe shoreline
of the bar and swim out into
what feels to me like
shark infested waters

Slowly I begin to learn
the names of the game

Dyke
Femme
Stone butch
Kiki

This last said in snide derision
of those who didn't know
who they were yet

Everyone acting out
the rules of roles
blindly toeing the gender line
aping the lives of our very own
cage keepers

Months of disappointment pass
femme's looking at me blankly
not getting my interest in them
until I finally give up and select
the smallest
least threatening
of available dykes
and take her home

Like a long caged hawk
set free
I soar into the sun
am consumed
transformed
into
Me

POWER OF CREATION

A spire reaches
for the sky
a rocket soars
beyond the eye

Yet nothing
could ever reach so high
as the flame we light together
with every glance
every sigh

At first a glowing ember
nesting in our hearts
quietly smoldering just as
every wildfire starts

But soon blazing
toward the treetops
devouring reason
in its raging

Now I lie here in your arms and wonder
will we leave the world in cinders
raze all within our path

Like two shooting stars colliding
with the power of creation
a new galaxy is formed
revolving round each other
Sammie and Kath

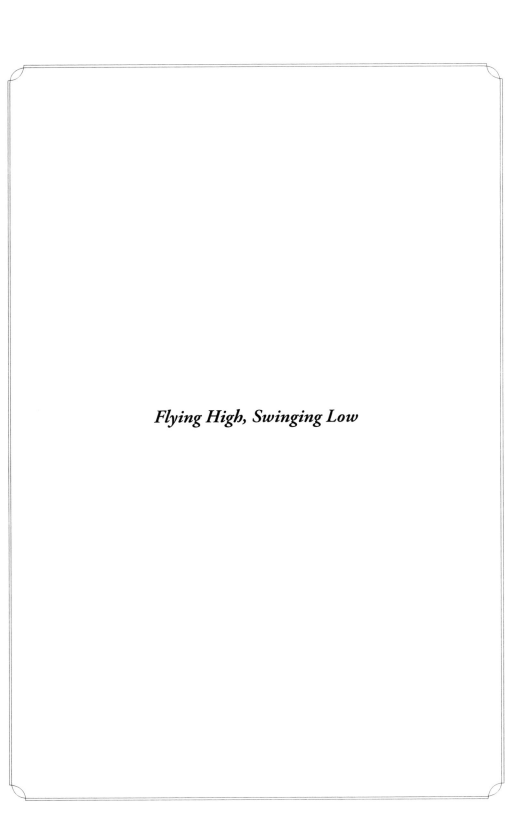

Flying High, Swinging Low

SECRETS AND LIES

So sweet
easy going
Southern Comfort
ever flowing

Yet I still feed
a secret craving
still need sex
with men
on the side

A hunger
growling
I am a wild beast prowling
stalking the thrill
of the hunt
the climatic passion
of the kill

I select
Seduce
Pounce
Capture
Devour

Back seat seconds
of stolen rapture

Two years pass
eating secrets
burying the broken bones
of lies

I awake one day to find
my sharp shovel of deception
has dug a deep hole
into my own heart

Love leaks out
and dies

FLIGHT

Drowning
in bitter tears
despairing
of my dreams

I race away from love
and all my many fears

Running blind
to love
and deaf
to my own heart's
screams

HUNGER

Soon
heartbreak
turns to
hunger

The starving
demanding to be fed

Trembling in my web conveys
a willing victim coming
into my parlor
soon into my bed

One of a couple
flying solo
ready to break the thin thread
of promises
she's made

I can feel the pheromones floating
intoxicating scent drifting like a mist
around our heads
luring us both
into an age-old dance

I pour her a drink
light a joint
read her porn
the words weaving
an easy bridge
to cross

Soon
her clothes and ring
are gone
with neither of us
measuring their loss

We become
wild mustangs racing
through a burning night
no one
owns

SWING SET

Frankie takes me down
to a dungeon
red velvet walls
harnessed slings dangling
from mirrored ceiling
sex hanging heavy, senses reeling

Bottom tied to a wooden cross
while a Top stands ready
tight red leather bodice
tall black boots
long black whip
pain somehow become
appealing

Adults only playground
swinger set
orgasmic orgies
ménage à trois
no boundaries
no fence
easy slide down
into decadence

In the back room
I lean far out over
green felt-covered table
long hard woody
held tight in hand

Red lace blouse
falling forward reveals
firm round breasts
unfettered
by modesty

I revel in my power
have my pick
of pricks
free home trial
king sized cannons
delayed firing
sex machines
never tiring

I come again
  and again
  and smile

IN WITH THE IN CROWD

At long last
I'm finally in
with the in crowd
finally got the message
clear and loud

Dicks want one thing
Janes another
so do what you want
just don't tell
mother

It's true what they say
men are from Mars
women from Venus
so you're shit out of luck
if you ain't got a penis

It's a man's world out there
no matter where you go
the rules remain the same
so just know
the only way for a girl to play and win
is to beat them at
their own game

SEX

Not love
comfort
honor
cherish
fidelity or
Happily Ever After

So look sharp
ya swabbies
listen well
get it right

If you want to sail
these treacherous seas of life
best batten down the hatches
and seal your heart up tight
in skepticism and lots
of black
latex

HARNESSED PASSIONS

Now that I know
what they look like
I recognize a dyke
at work

Soon
we are sitting in a bar
she pointing out to me
the butches
what are packin'
making up for
what a woman's
lacking

Has to spell it out at first
until I can see
that familiar bulge
where a man's would be

Mind spins like a dreidel top
I am Alice lost in a land
where so many things
are not what they are seeming
her words give strap on and harness
a whole new meaning

Just like cucumbers
it's not a matter of luck
you don't have to guess
at what you're getting
or worry you'll get stuck
with far more or less
than would be fitting

Much later that night
I'm thrilled to discover
I can have the best
of both worlds
under the covers

Even when I'm straight
about being with men
Jody says fine
we'll just be lovers
no need for lies
no need for strings

But there are still
some things
that I don't share
after all
isn't that what
freedom
really
means

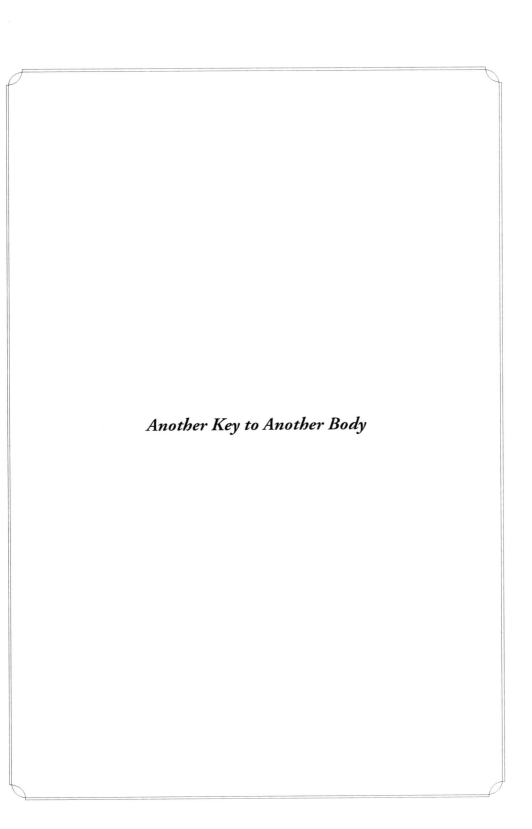

Another Key to Another Body

BEND OR BREAK

Late night
early morning
not sure which
Frankie and I've
been downing shots here
since six

She staggers back
from the rest room
reeling like a novice sailor
in high seas
her careening passage
as dangerous to dancers
as a swinging boom
during hard tack

Can't get her to stop
can't get her keys
doesn't work to get angry
doesn't work to say please

Finally
I give up
roll my eyes
at the bartender
pay my tab
leave her sitting at a table
with some guys

How I am able
to get home myself
God only knows
I stumble up the stairs
fall into bed
still wearing all my clothes
brain checked out
before pillow
hits head

Only to be reeled rudely awake
by Jody's gruff command
and rougher shake

Her sharp look pierces
voice cuts cold
as she snaps one crisp name
and hands me the phone

She has always known about Frankie
but like her love for me
it has always gone
unspoken

But the tight strained voice
on the other end
not Frankie's instead
that of her long-time girlfriend

The crash was head-on
Frankie nearly died
she's in the ER now
both legs broken
and calling out your name

I am book-ended
between two lovers
with really no choice
I rush to be by her side

Stench of alcohol fills the room
Frankie lies there swathed in bandages
and gloom

Limp and ragged like a disgarded doll
crushed legs encased
in plaster casts
close but far away
I hear a doctor say

Won't know the damage
to her brain
until the coma's past

But what is painfully clear
to all of us
is that Frankie will never ever
be the same

Her partner Dannie's eyes meet mine
her expression one of loss
not blame

Even now wanting what is best
for this woman she holds so dear
willing to let go
no matter what
her cost

But through a blur of unshed tears
I concede my love to her
knowing it's the price a cheater
will always pay

I kiss and release Frankie's hand
for one last time
turn
and walk
away

RAGE

Returning to an empty house
evidence of rage flung
all about

Bent and twisted
picture frames
lying
on floor

Glass broken out by the impact
of heartbreak
sharp shards kissing jagged pieces
of a shattered vase

Vibrant flowers given
just the day before
strewn throughout the wreckage
dying
like stranded fish out of water

Edges brown & curled
from the loss of love
that once fed them

Swept by fear of her return
my father back in female form
I race through the rooms
throwing everything I own
into one ragged pillowcase

Last of all I leave
my heart-shaped key
on the nightstand by the bed
right on top of the note she left for me
one I now know far too well
Go with her
and go
to hell

ANOTHER KEY

Paint's hardly dry on my last escape
when my eyes meet another's
across a crowded room

Attraction crackles heavy in the air
like summer lightning on a clear day
thumping beat of bass standing in for
thunder's boom

Five drinks later we skip romance
in favor of *vertical sex*
otherwise known as
dirty dancing
prelude to a long
and passionate night

Late the next morning
lying warm and languid in her bed
not remembering what I have
or haven't said
I offer my now-standard disclaimer about men
but Diane just grins
picks up the phone
calls a male friend over
to join us
in sin

Two days later
I drive up to her house
in a U-Haul truck
thinking to myself
I really should buy stock

Reaching her door I turn
yet another
heart-shaped key
in yet another
lonely
lock

HONEYMOON

Ah the blissful honeymoon
knowing I've finally got it right
loving passion
through the night

Weekends hangin' at the bar
drinking
dancing
playing pool
fights in the parking lot over keys
no drunk driving now a rule

A friend of hers comes to visit
a drab and stern young-old woman
I find of little interest
until I hear she's a Dominitrist

Lust ignites
that old familiar craving
for kinky sex
and wild delights

I squirrel away her number
against a future
hunger

JUST ANOTHER BODY

I wake one day to the news
Jerry's downtown raving
to his muse

Far faster than a heartbeat
I'm there and back again
throw him into bed to get
that old familiar rush
that old familiar hit

For me he's still
the best drug out there
on the street

But soon I realize
while the sex is hot
somehow
it's not

His body's movements
rote
his penis there
but mind remote

I lie there and wonder
Does he even remember
I was once his wife
or does he think
I'm just another body
left there
for him to use

FAMILIAR FLIGHT

After sex Jerry lies limp
as a newborn child
I have to haul him up
bathe
feed
drive him back downtown
put him on a bus

So hard to see
there's nothing left
of him
or
us

I drive slowly back home to share
the sadness of my husband's fate
but am stunned and shocked to feel
a flash fire of temper flare
spewing forth
molten words
of hate

Rage roaring so loud
can't be sure what is said
is she furious that it was him
without her
or in our bed

Stumbling from her fury
I run
still not really knowing
just what it is
I've done

Simply fleeing fear
and what seems my destiny
racing blindly into the night
in all too familiar
flight

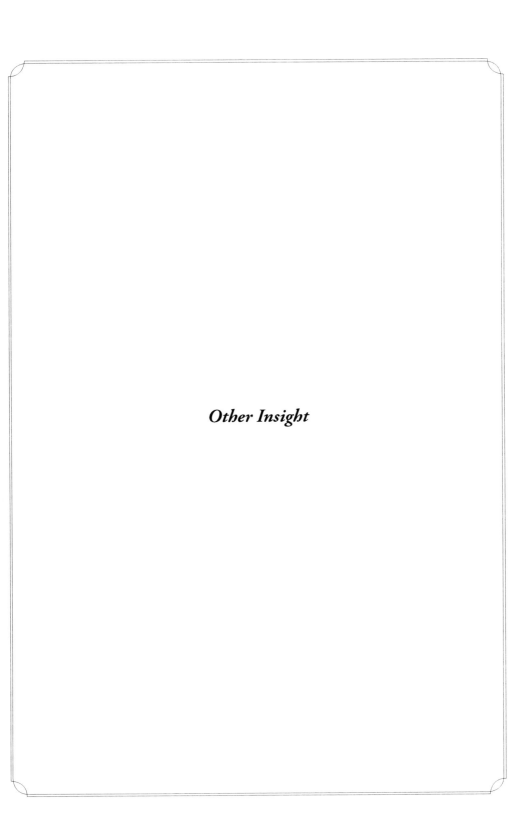

Other Insight

ANOTHER DOOR

I've barely closed the last before
I race away toward
yet another door

Staggering down
stone stairs
dungeon's gate
I raise my fist
and knock

Feet wanting just
to flee
faint heart
flying after
closing eyes
breathing deep
I tell them both
to wait

Heavy booted step
cry
of creaking floor
scream
of rusty lock

Trembling
I stand with naked soul
before my fate

Iron-studded and strapped
door swings open
framing in black
the well remembered dark
Dominatrix

Doubtful eyes gaze down
skeptical of my smallness
lipstick
bouffant hair
painted nails

Yet seems still to see
a place
where wild rage swells
in me

Smiles knowingly
stands aside and bids me enter
motioning to her bed

Shedding clothes
like chameleon skin
I rush in
where angels fear to tread
hear behind me
the door to Dante's heaven
close
again

PARTNERED IN PAIN

Knick-knack
Tally whack
Give your dog a bone
This old crone
comes marching home

The silly children's song
looped endlessly through my mind
keeping time I suppose
with the steady rise and fall of my arm
vertical metronome

Leather belt
solid smack
tender flesh
angry welt

Partnered in pain
we move to a steady rhythm
suffering slowly metered out
twisted love kissing skin
like acid rain

Short on sympathy
I tower tall
flush with the power
of it all

Somehow
remake the past
tortured memories
recast

I only do
what I am told
she truly the one
with all control

How many
how hard
where
when
stop
no
do it again

Pain or pleasure
perhaps both
in equal measure

ANOTHER BROKEN HEART

Like beaten gold
love wears thin

Perversion
just another hopeless
diversion

Neurotic ecstasy
not what
I was led to believe

Instead I find
just another broken heart
worn
on yet another
tattered sleeve

Just another legacy
of childhood
wrought by just another parent
who could
or should
have given more
or less

Dooming yet another
grown up child
to a life of pain
and perpetual
distress

Playing out
just another twisted
Act of Contrition
given for some real
or imagined
sin of omission

Forgive me father
for I have sinned
I seem to do the wrong thing
in your eyes
no matter what I mean
or intend

Do not despair my daughter
the devil leads all lambs
to slaughter

The road to hell is paved
with good intentions
not even angels hold
exemption

But these punishments I meter out
will absolve and lead you back
to God's eternal love
and redemption

With relief I welcome
her extended trip
but she has hardly shut the door
before the terror of aloneness
chokes me
in its deadly grip

Grabbing heart-shaped key
I lock the door and flee
pick up just another woman
in just another bar

Race home
load car
gone
long before
guilt
or doubt
can dawn

Hitting Bottom, Stepping Up

LAY LADY LAY [7]

Ruby sang
right into my eyes
though pronoun wrong
still
our song

Waitress by day
singer by night
dark
exotic
raven hair flowing
yet soul sad
with knowing

Sitting alone
in the darkened bar
I see two men
looking at her
looking at me

They smile
with approving winks
slide on over
to buy us drinks

Though clearly loath
Ruby joins us on her break
while they grin broadly
and make it clear
they wanna take us
both

Ah come on gals
they beg and plead
We'll make sure you get
what you need

Now I'm always up
for getting down
but Ruby says no
with an angry frown
returns to the stage

They buy more shots
dissolving resistance
blurring thoughts
mind begins to disengage

Mourning sun
scorches blindingly bright
into swollen eyes
body wedged tight
between two guys
I cringe and wonder
what I've done

Wiggle
slip
slide
over silken sheets
ooze out the end
of a massive bed

Crawl around
cold marble floor
searching for clothes
and my fallen head
finally slither
out the door

Home at last but
dead bolt locked
welcome mat taken in
shutters shut

Not even shocked
I turn away
knowing
there's really nothing
I can say

TRAIN WRECK

Love has left the station
yet another time
left me standing on the platform
without a single dime

So very tired of being lost
I realize
I've got to find another way
no matter what the cost

Tell my family that I'm dying
just can't keep on trying

No knowing
where I'm going

Only that my life's
a train wreck
got to get it back
on track

SHRINK WRAPPED

Once again
I stare blankly
at the shrink
scared
of what she's gonna think

But hoping
she can figure out my stuff
why just loving some One
is never ever
enough

I break everything
that I touch
every life
every heart
always want
too much

Never matters
the love I feel
I always think it is
but it isn't
real

Never happy
with the work I do
what my life's about
I haven't a clue

Mind
Body
Spirit
Sick
Through and through

Hour's end
she looks at me
and speaks
with the ringing voice
of prophecy

Heal yourself
and you'll discover
how to help others
who were lost
like you

Stunned by this riddled sphinx
not able or daring to question
the right or wisdom of her
holy exemption
I rise and stride
across the hardwood floor

Reach out a trembling hand
to open
one last door
take the first step
onto
a new path of
redemption

On to a
New Beginning

Dear Reader,

I sincerely hope that you have survived your "reckless ride through the wild currents" of Sammie's life unscathed, but not unchanged. Thank you for sharing this portion of Sammie's journey and I hope that you will join us for its conclusion, Forged in Fire — *Redemption* to be released in 2016. I hope that Sammie's story and my Notes have given you a better understanding of the impact of childhood abuse, as well as some useful resources for healing and growth.

Girl on Fire has followed Sammie's life from the ages of twelve to twenty-five. *Redemption* will continue Sammie's journey of self-discovery and healing. Here are two entries from Sammie's notebook, *Forged in Fire — Redemption.*

ICY WINDS OF CHANGE

Shivering
I balance precariously
on a thin strand of hope

Buffeted
by icy winds of change
and wait
for them to blow me over

To
one side
or
the other

SEEDS

Some seeds need
a shallow bed
others
deep

Some blazing sun
others
dark
to sleep

Some lives lie
ever fallow while
others
flourish

Some nothing
others
little
will nourish

Some famine
strengthens
others
doom

Some simply time
others
Fire
to bloom

Companion Notes

Forged in Fire
Girl on Fire

You have chosen to join Sammie on her journey of reflection through a life that was often painful and challenging. Whether you are an Adult Survivor of Child Abuse (ASCA), a friend or partner of an ASCA, a therapist, or simply an avid reader, these Companion Notes are offered to support and guide you in gaining a deeper understanding, not just of Sammie's unique story, but of the impact abusive childhood experiences can have can have on the development of any child's personality, long-term mental health, and ongoing happiness.

These Notes are not meant to be a comprehensive coverage of the impact of childhood neglect and abuse, but rather a direct reference to the particular "symptoms" being demonstrated by Sammie, the heroine of this journey, in each segment of her story. As you gain a better understanding of the forces that drive Sammie, you might also gain deeper insight into your own behavior or that of someone you care about. You may even want to take what you learn here into your own therapy or use it to talk with a loved one about their own experience. The resources cited here may also serve as guides to pursue specific issues more fully.

For the Survivor: It is my hope that, as you walk through the fire with Sammie, you will let its flames ignite your own healing and growth.

VOICES: Survivor, Writer, Inner (Ghost) Child
Pages 1 through 4

Forged – presents an overview of Sammie's journey
Speak For Me – introduces the concept of a "Wounded Inner Child"
Ghost Child – depicts the instinctual psychological draw toward healing and wholeness

Forged – As an adult, Sammie tells us that she has been, "thrust into the fire/ravaged and consumed", her soul, "burned down to bone" and yet she has survived, "one small ember shone." Beyond that, she has not only survived but is now thriving, coming to see herself as a "tempered spirit born anew" "forged to show others The Way."

Psychologically, Sammie has transformed the hurt and anger associated with her past into an appreciation of how her experiences have strengthened and shaped who she is in the present. Spiritually, she has transitioned from a Self identity as "victim" or an inherently "bad seed," to one of "Survivor" or "spiritual warrior" — someone who has found meaning and purpose in a difficult life journey.

Encouragingly, one notable study of resilience – a person's ability to resist or 'bounce back' from adverse life experiences — showed that forty-nine percent of adults who were abused as children met the criteria for resiliency.[8] We can take heart in knowing that it is never too late to start the journey to healing and that there is always more to be gained from continuing it.

Speak For Me and *Ghost Child* – Sammie, as the writer of this book, struggles with self-doubt and fear of failure, but her psyche's need to be healed draws her inexorably back to the "wounded inner child" who must be heard. "Large sunken eyes in ancient face looked slowly up at me and she whispered, 'Speak for me.'"

John Bradshaw introduced the term "wounded inner child" to symbolize those parts of personality that become developmentally "stuck" and need to be healed in order for someone to have a healthy, happy and well-functioning life.[9] His works are excellent resources.

Several famous theorists have advanced the idea that we are inherently or innately drawn to heal our psychological "wounds" and reach our full potential as human beings.[10] The fact that you've chosen to read this book may be an indication of your own readiness to begin or continue that journey.

Through Journal Therapy or reflective writing, you can gain mental and emotional clarity, validate your experiences and come to a deeper understanding of yourself.[11] As Sammie's own wounded inner or Ghost Child encourages, "Heal me, I will grow."

Home Sweet Home
Pages 7 through 12

Craacckk! – introduces the concept of compartmentalization
Empty Cup – depicts the emotionally absent/neglectful parent
The Only Touch – presents a present, but abusive parent
Kill Zone – reveals home as a dangerous place to be

In *Craacckk!* – Sammie employs a common coping mechanism – the ability to compartmentalize, or separate from conscious awareness, the painful thoughts and feelings associated with her home life so that she can participate in and enjoy outside activities. As she says, "*When not at home, life was good.*" Unfortunately, this ability to compartmentalize pain often means that adults around an abused child have no inkling of their situation, thus delaying or preventing help.

We can also see that Sammie's physical prowess and skill provide her with vital peer connection; healthy adult contact, support and encouragement (in the unseen coach) and are a powerful source of self-esteem.

Empty Cup and ***The Only Touch*** – Sammie shares with us
her deep sense of emotional abandonment by her mother, "my
mother holds an empty cup," and her resultant strong attachment
to her father – despite his physical abuse, "he is my hero, except
when he is mad."

Children who experience emotional neglect suffer at least
as much, if not more so, than if they were being physically
assaulted.[12] However, as an adult, you may tend to minimize or
not be consciously aware of the very real impact that emotional
neglect has had on you.

The "trauma bonding" that occurs between Sammie and her
father is common in both children and adults when they are
unable to escape abusive circumstances.[13] An abuser may be
the only source of parental attachment (something children
desperately need) and he/she may give rewards and comfort
at times, causing you to feel a confusing mix of fear, love,
gratitude and loyalty towards him/her.[14] You may even still be
struggling with these feelings as an adult and find it hard to set
limits with an unhealthy parent.

Kill Zone – Sammie and all of her siblings demonstrate one of
the four basic roles children take on in dysfunctional families – that
of the Invisible Child (the other three are the Hero, Mascot,
and Scapegoat).[15] In this poem, we can see that her home is
a dangerous place, where she can only retreat to "the relative
safety of my bedroom/the torture chamber where I hide."

You might have taken one of these four roles on as a child and
carried it into adulthood or you may have shifted to another
as circumstances changed. It is important to realize that what
you perceive as your innate, unchangeable "personality" might
actually be a learned coping mechanism – which, of course, can be
unlearned and replaced with more effective behaviors.

Heaven's Light Dies — introduces the concept of spiritual wounding
Growin Up — sexual molest compounds emotional neglect and physical abuse
Crystal Shards — spiritual death; the loss of faith in a benevolent, protective "God"

Heaven's Light Dies — Retrospective studies of ASCA's have reported that, as children, they felt abandoned and betrayed by a God they were taught to believe would protect them if they were good.[16] When they tried hard to be "good," but were punished anyway, they blamed themselves — feeling ashamed, guilty, worthless, and depressed.[17] Many also abandoned their beliefs and practices, while continuing to harbor deep resentments and anger towards their "God."

As part of your own healing journey, it may be important for you to address and resolve "God" anger and find some form of spirituality that can give you comfort and support.

Growin Up — Sexual abuse deeply compounds the effects of emotional/physical abuse, almost doubling the odds of problems in all areas of life functioning, such as substance abuse, mental and relational health.[18]

Crystal Shards — Representative of both the death of spiritual belief and, potentially, physical death. Child and adolescent suicide is a shocking reality in America, where 4,900 children chose to end their own lives (1/5 of those being between five and fourteen) in 2011.[19]

Chronic depression is common among ASCA's and may be so much a part of you that you don't even recognize it as a treatable condition. Evaluation by a trained specialist, such as a psychiatrist, might change your life for the better.

Snapshots – represents repressed memories and traumatic amnesia
The Long Sleep – subconscious processing of fear through creative expression
Rebellion – conversion of fear and depression into rage
Breaking Back – development of passive-aggressive behavior

Snapshots – ASCA's often have little or no memory of their childhood (repressed memories, traumatic amnesia, or dissociation)[20] and traumatic events may or may not ever be recalled; however, they can continue to deeply affect our lives. Thankfully, healing and growth can still be achieved in the absence of these memories.[21]

The Long Sleep – Creative expression represents the psyche's efforts to find meaning in life's experiences, gain relief from overwhelming emotions or trauma, resolve conflicts and problems, enrich daily life, and achieve an increased sense of well-being.[22] "Expressive arts therapy," involves the use of various kinds of creative art (music, art, movement, and other art forms) and may be a very enjoyable and beneficial form of help to seek at some point in your recovery efforts.[23]

Rebellion and Breaking Back – Abused children often have problems with fear, anxiety, depression, anger and hostility, aggression, self-destructive behavior, feelings of isolation and stigma, poor self-esteem, difficulty in trusting others, substance abuse, and, for those who experience sexual abuse as well, sexually inappropriate behavior and/or sexual maladjustment (under-or-overly sexual).[24]

From a childhood roles perspective, a shift from depression to anger/rage may signify a shift from being an "Invisible Child" to a "Scapegoat." If you recognize any of these symptoms within yourself, therapy can help you resolve them so that you can enjoy a happier, more functional life.

Young Love
Pages 29 through 39

Love Scores a Ringer – efforts to transfer attachment needs to a new love object
Shattered – reinforcement of the core belief, "I am not loveable."
Hiding in Open Sight – progression of molest and the "flight" response
A Wild, Wild Furie – conversion of depression to rage

Love Scores a Ringer – Sammie's behavior depicts one of the attachment styles characteristic of ASCA's, an insecure or preoccupied relational focus characterized by extreme dependency and clinginess.[25]

Shattered – Individuals with an insecure attachment style may feel especially distraught at the end of a relationship, because they blame themselves for its problems – just as they do their own abuse.[26]

Sexual abuse can result in a sexualized identity, as in "I am my sexuality" or "My sexuality is the most important thing about me" and result in earlier and more active sexual behavior than the norm.[27]

Hiding in Open Sight and *A Wild, Wild Furie* – While Sammie expresses anger internally, her actual external behavior is one of "flight" from immediate threat.[28] You may want to consider which survival response (fight, flight, or freeze) you chose, whether or not it is still operating in your life and, if so, explore the extent to which it's working or not working for you.

Sex—The Good, The Bad and The Ugly
Pages 43 through 54

The Bad One – depicts typical symptomatic behaviors of abused children; hypersexuality

Bitter Victory – choice point between continued victimhood or rebellion
A Little Death – creative expression as an emotional outlet
Soaring – Abandoned Child Syndrome; porn impact
Broken Silence – breaking the silence; venting mother-anger; rule breaking
Just as Well – internalization of parental criticism; abuser-victim symbiosis; repetitive compulsive/trauma reenactment and revictimization

The Bad One depicts some of the typical acting out or symptomatic behaviors of abused children. Sammie tells us that she is, ".... the Bad One now—failing grades, always in trouble, rageful," and that she ".... got caught stealing a BB gun for a boy I hardly knew." She has obviously transitioned from her immobilizing depression into energized, but delinquent, behavior. Paired or group delinquency may represent an abused child's desperate efforts to form a substitute family and feel worthwhile. Unfortunately, these common symptoms of abuse may only add to a child's problems and worsen her already low self-esteem.

Sammie also refers to one of the strongest indicators of child sexual abuse — sexual preoccupation in the form of excessive masturbation, "...and my body is aflame insatiably driving me to feed the ravenous hunger gnawing there between my legs."

Bitter Victory reflects the typical progression of incest from molestation to intercourse and depicts the child's limited options in responding to the abuse— either continued passive victimhood or aggressive rebellion. Sammie's decision to actively seek out sex with a peer rather than allow her father to take her virginity, "I'll be dammed if he will be the first!" is apparently a choice made by many molested children—as studies show that childhood sexual abuse is strongly associated with having sex at a younger age[29] and with teenage pregnancy.[30]

A Little Death, like The Long Sleep, is another example of Sammie's subconscious efforts to find emotional relief from the intolerable anxiety of her situation. In this poem, she creates a maternal place of refuge that does not exist in her real world, "Mother Tree," and hope for eventual freedom from her pain. The metamorphous from caterpillar to butterfly may be representative of her lingering desire for death as a release from her painful (mortal) existence to an idyllic (divine) one, "I spread my wings and fly."

In *Soaring*, we witness Sammie's desperate need to find connection and love outside of her home, as well as her distorted belief that sex equals love, "nothing else really matters now that I am loved." We also see how a molest victim can be sexually precocious in some ways, but sexually naive in others. When Sammie experiences "a feeling like he's peeing inside me," she reveals her total lack of knowledge regarding sperm and ejaculation.

Soaring also reveals the impact pornography has had on Sammie's attitudes towards sex; it has established preconceptions and expectations of what sex is like, which can set the stage for confusion and disappointment in real life encounters- "no pounding passion, no piercing screams of ecstasy, no hour long orgasms."[31] While Sammie does not yet respond in this way, dissatisfaction, frustration and even anger towards a partner can result when such expectations are not met.[32]

In *Broken Silence*, Sammie is finally able to disclose the molest to her mother, "Dad's been messin with me for years," while also venting her anger at being judged for her own sexual behavior and not being protected from her father, "I don't wanna hear nothin out of you."

In general, childhood abuse can cause a child to "throw out" whatever "rule book" of ethics and values abusive parents and society as a whole (as represented by schools, churches and other authority figures) have tried to instill in her. Studies have found that adult CSAs are still angry towards God and that they tend to have little, if any, form of religious practice compared to non-survivors.[33] Other studies have shown that children who have experienced abuse are nine times more likely to be involved in criminal activities later in life.[34]

Just as Well depicts both the internalization of parental criticism, "I wasn't doing so good there [school] anyway, too stupid I guess," and the impaired learning ability (reflected by academic underachievement) that is common among children living in a dysfunctional home environment.[35] It also depicts the symbiotic or trauma bonding that can develop between a molest victim and her abuser, "liked using his power on the one hand, felt awful on the other," a situation that can further damage the integrity and self-esteem of a victim.

Such early patterning of relational dysfunction can result in an unconscious repetition compulsion or trauma reenactment which causes the adult incest survivor to use sex as a way to get needs met—even to the point of recreating the original abuse in some form again and again. Studies of adult incest survivors consistently show a higher than average incidence of domestic violence, rape, unwanted sexual advances by authority figures, enticement into pornography, self-harm behavior and prostitution.[36]

Child Parent
Pages 57 through 66

Solitary Confinement – Sammie enjoys the safety of her escape, but is shocked by the physical changes of her pregnancy
Game Time – a toast to delivery
Light Blue Eyes – post-delivery delirium
Two Children and a Child – Sammie and Trey struggle with their new parenting role
Dark Shadow – angrophobia, fear of one's own anger; anger issues and abuse; fear of inheriting parents' abusive tendencies
Dishonorable Discharge – abandoning own child; rebuilding shattered self-esteem

In this set of poems, we see how Sammie struggles to understand and cope with her new parenting role. Studies have found that young CSA mothers are more likely to struggle with anger issues and be abusive towards their children than non-CSA mothers[37], as is reflected in **Dark Shadow** when Sammie loses control and causes "a lifelong scar bearing my name." **Dark Shadow** also portrays a common fear of the adult abuse survivor—that she will "inherit" her parents' abusive tendencies. "I feel the dark shadow of my father falling over me." Ironically, this fear leads Sammie, in **Dishonorable Discharge**, to "abandon" her own daughter at home while she goes to work. However, in doing so, she begins to rebuild her shattered self-esteem. "I am amazed to discover I can actually learn to make change… maybe I'm not such a 'stupid girl' after all."

Trauma & its Wake
Pages 69 through 74

Regret – Trey triggers Sammie's "abandonment" issues
Seven Come Eleven – "sex addiction" behavior; damaged values and boundaries
Empty House – flight; protecting her daughter
Alone – classically conditioned association between being alone and danger; alcohol as escape

In **Regret**, we see that Sammie's husband is also struggling with the consequences of being a young parent. He is, "too tired to give me much," and treats his daughter as if she were "invisible." Unfortunately, in using the coping mechanism of emotional and physical withdrawal from both his wife and child, "Trey" triggers Sammie's "abandonment" issues and she "acts out."

Seven Come Eleven demonstrates the characteristics of traumatic sexualization[38] — Sammie's sense of self-worth and identity have become sexualized. When the 7-Eleven man "begins to flirt," she becomes, "high on the power," of a man's attraction to her. And, in classic "sex addiction" behavior, she uses the excitement of engaging in illicit sex as a coping mechanism for her boredom and feelings of abandonment by her husband.

Sammie's behavior also reveals her abuse-related lack of values and boundaries, in that she seems completely unconcerned about being unfaithful. Her comments also demonstrate the development of a common feature of sex addiction—a dual or secret sexual life, "I've grown used to keeping hidden the forbidden."

In *Empty House*, we see examples of Sammie's fierce protectiveness toward her daughter, combined with her predominate survival mechanism—flight. She has had no models for healthy communication between adults and her life experience has taught her that when violence begins, it will only get worse. Having been unable to escape her own childhood abuse, she is determined to protect her daughter from a similar fate in the only way she knows how—flight.

Alone demonstrates both Sammie's "abandonment issues" and her subconscious, classically conditioned association between being alone and danger. In fact, she is, "overwhelmed by the terror of being alone," to the point of feeling "insane" and resorts to alcohol so she won't "have to feel the pain," won't, "have to think."

These kinds of conditioned emotional responses (CERs) can also be triggered by the sudden raising of a hand, yelling, the slamming of doors, or by strong emotions such as terror or rage, resulting in strong instinctual reactions (flight, fight or freeze).[39]

Bad Seed
Pages 77 through 85

Stones – social incompetence, poor peer relationships and peer rejection
Supernova – conditioned expectations of porn; intensity equals intimacy; sex as a coping mechanism
Hole in the Wall – self-blame; trauma bonding
Unfit – self-blame

Stones depicts the social difficulties suffered by child abuse victims — social incompetence, poor peer relationships and peer rejection. "I can still see scornful judgment in their eyes."[40] The experience of peer rejection can further damage the abuse victim by compounding her sense of aloneness, her low self-esteem and feelings of insecurity – resulting in depression or aggression – and as a child develops, heightened sensitivity to rejection.[41]

In *Supernova*, Sammie finally experiences the kind of romantic encounter and "mind-blowing sex" she has read about in her father's pornography and that she has been "conditioned" to associate with love—a "passion that has no boundaries, no rules, no walls." She also discovers a second coping mechanism – sex – that allows her to escape her constant negative emotions to "become only feeling."

In *Hole in the Wall* and *Unfit*, Sammie experiences yet another traumatic event and once again blames herself for the crisis. "I have only myself to blame." Ironically, as many adult survivors do, she turns to her abuser (father) for protection (trauma bonding).[42]

Sex, Drugs and Rock n' Roll
Pages 89 through 102

Purple Haze – drugs as another coping mechanism
Mad Mad World – displacement of unresolved anger
Missing in Action – another abandonment
Back into the Void – Abandoned Child Syndrome (ACS); flight defense
Ground Zero – ACS; the geographic cure
Arrested Development – premature aging; dawning awareness of sex addiction
Junkie – dawning awareness of sex addiction

In *Purple Haze* and *Mad Mad World*, Sammie adds yet another unhealthy coping mechanism to her emotional defense arsenal—drugs—and is able to "find release, a place to shelter, a place to hide." Research has consistently shown that survivors of childhood abuse are at increased risk to smoke cigarettes, abuse alcohol, and/or take illicit drugs during their lifetime.[43]

She also "displaces" her unresolved anger towards her parents (authority figures) onto what she perceives as equally unjust social issues (the Civil Rights Movement, Feminist and Labor movements), unconsciously attempting to assert power and effect change, thereby gaining some sense of control and self-esteem. "Hell no, he won't go to war."

In *Missing in Action*, Sammie suffers yet another abandonment by a "love object," but then discovers Jerry is schizophrenic—a concept she is ill-equipped to fully understand or factor into their relationship.

Back into the Void and *Ground Zero* depict the enduring and intense symptoms of "Abandoned Child Syndrome"—a profound experience of inner emptiness and disconnection from others, as well as a terror of being unloved or of being left alone. "I can feel myself falling back into the void."[44] In an instinctual flight from unbearable feelings, Sammie finds herself, "fleeing the deadly firestorm of burning memories" – what is known in the recovery field as a geographic cure.

Arrested Development illustrates the emotional premature aging of the incest survivor, "…. though the same age I feel old," as well as Sammie's multiple addictions (alcohol, marijuana and sex), "smoke dope, have no-strings-sex with strangers." Numerous theorists have proposed that childhood sexual abuse may lead to the development of sex and love addiction and a high percentage of sex addicts seeking treatment do, in fact, report childhood sexual abuse.[45] *Arrested Development* is also a reference to the idea that individuals suffering from sex and love addiction are developmentally "stuck" in the "Eros" stage of relational love, finding it difficult to move on to the more mature and lasting form of love known as "agape."

Junkie reveals that while Sammie has some level of awareness that her irrational clinging to Jerry is unhealthy, she is still powerlessness to let him go, "even if he is mad as a hatter, I'm still a junkie and he's still my drug."

First Love — Last Straw
Pages 105 through 115

Settle In – attachment disorder with daughter; mother anger
Nasty Weather – revictimization; devaluation of self; learned helplessness; split between conscious defense mechanisms & unconscious emotional reactions; denial and minimization
Here in Absentia – mistrust generalizes to all men
Last Straw – coming out; sexual anorexia
Home – childhood attraction repressed due to fears
Eternity – desperate desire to love and be loved (ACS); idolized or rapturous love

With *Settle In* we see Sammie's attachment disorder—an emotional disconnect and lack of empathy for the needs of her daughter, "no going home first to see the kid." We also witness her continued bitterness towards her mother, "it's about time she was there for someone else for a change."

Theorists have speculated that incest survivors hold anger towards their mothers for "allowing" the abuse to occur and/or continue.[46] Other dynamics that I have encountered in my work with incest survivors include: 1) a belief that the mother did not care what happened to the child, 2) fear the child would not be believed and would be severely punished for lying, and 3) the child would be believed and therefore responsible for the dissolution of the family.

Nasty Weather is an example of revictimization, a common phenomenon in CSAs.[47] Revictimization may be related to a devaluation of self, "I start to worry I'll be a bother," and/or to learned helplessness. It also reflects the split between conscious defense mechanisms, "no harm, no foul" (denial or minimization of trauma impact) and true unconscious emotional reactions, "soul frozen solid, neither alive nor dead, hope fading slowly out of sight." Denial can prevent awareness of trauma symptoms, thereby delaying the seeking out of help to resolve trauma wounds; it can also interfere with the ability to form healthy relationships and may contribute to physical ailments.[48]

In *Last Straw* and *Home* Sammie makes the shift from a heterosexual to a homosexual identity. While the incest, recurrent abandonment and revictimization, as depicted in *Nasty Weather*, and *Last Straw*, all seem to suggest that Sammie has been "driven into homosexuality," many factors can affect how an individual's sexual identity is developed—including internal processes, societal forces, and family pressures.[49] While the majority of studies have found no direct causal link between childhood sexual abuse and later identification as a non-heterosexual adult,[50] some studies have found a twenty-five to fifty-percent higher incidence of CSA among non-heterosexual individuals.[51]

It is also important to note that, through the psychological process of generalization, an incest survivor may become adverse, even phobic, to engaging in sex with a member of the same gender that abused them.[52] And, in extreme cases, a survivor may develop sexual anorexia and be completely avoidant of any sexual activity with either gender.[53]

In *Eternity,* we witness Sammie's desperate need to love and be loved, "through all Eternity." This is a common trait among those with Abandoned Child Syndrome (ACS)[54] and unfortunately, at this early stage in her life, Sammie is only capable of what the Greeks described as the "Eros" form of love—a passionate and intense love that often triggers an emotional "high." It is this high that "sex and love addicts" chase through serial relationships, promiscuity, and affairs.

Trauma and Rebirth
Pages 119 through 124

Interlude – more abandonment, core wounding and core beliefs

Dad Defeated – trauma bonding, ambivalence and lack of closure

Formal Grief – shame and self-blame; "I'm defective"

Here Be Dragons – disconnection from family; Sammie's fear of completely cutting loose from her old life

In *Interlude*, Sammie experiences yet another abandonment by someone she loves and plunges once more into the deep dark well of core wounding (ACS). Her abject pain at this loss reveals two of her core beliefs about herself, "I am not loveable" and "I will always be abandoned." These are reflected in her last stanza, "I stand condemned to eternal solitude."

Dad Defeated and *Formal Grief* both demonstrate Sammie's trauma bonding with her father and her ambivalence towards his death. She experiences, "an odd regret warring with relief." On the one hand, she is finally free of his abuse, but on the other, she will never have resolution or closure with him (he has never confessed to his molest or asked her for forgiveness), nor will she ever be vindicated in the truth of her abuse. She is left to carry her shame and self-blame, reflected in the line, "people must think I'm heartless, too."

In addition, as long as her father was alive, some part of her could believe that, although warped, at least one of her parents "loved" and wanted her. Now, she is left with only a "deep emptiness inside" (the abandonment wound). Consequently, Sammie is left to wonder, "...if justice is truly mine."

While it is not always possible to obtain "closure" with an abandoning or abusive parent, it is possible to resolve this issue through self-help or professional resources. Harold H. Bloomfield's, *Making Peace with Your Parents,* is an excellent source of further study.

In *Here Be Dragons*, Sammie continues to struggle with feelings of loss for her father, as well as with her deep sense of disconnection from the rest of her family, having become the **Bad One** now, or scapegoat. Dysfunctional families are often characterized by this lack of healthy attachment and the Incest Survivor, in particular, may feel estranged from other members due to the secret she feels forced to hold.

Ironically, with her father's death, she no longer has to fear his wrath if he were to discover her new sexual orientation and she feels she has nothing more to lose with the rest of her family. As terrifying as this new, uncharted territory might be, Sammie knows she cannot return to a, "life I can no more pretend has ever served me well," and realizes that she must, "launch myself not knowing if what lies at voyage's end be heaven or be hell."

Down the Rabbit Hole
Pages 126 through 130

Landfall – Sammie enters the gay subculture; confronts her stereotypes; cognitive dissonance
Green Door – subculture shock
Ends Up – subculture shock

This set of poems depicts Sammie's entry into a subculture of life that she has only read about in her father's pornography books and heard condemned by her church. She is immediately challenged to confront her stereotypes regarding gay men and struggles with the cognitive dissonance (the mental stress or discomfort experienced when someone is confronted by new information that conflicts with existing beliefs, ideas, or values) this creates.

Weird World Wonderland
Pages 133 through 144

Just Human Ways – oppression rage
Lavender Door – entering the lesbian subculture
Rocky Passage – accepted at last
Lesbian Land – lesbian subculture mimics the dominant society
Shark Bait – choosing a subculture identity
Power of Creation – love addiction and Eros love

In *Just Human Ways*, we see Sammie expressing oppression rage, a deep-seated emotional response to repeated experiences of degradation and devaluation.[55] On a subconscious level, she is attempting to join with her new oppressed community and throw off her deeply embedded victim identity, although we can see by her last line, "yet I still have to wonder, will there ever be a day when it sings for me," that she is very skeptical that this will come to pass.

The next four poems in the set, *Lavender Door*, *Rocky Passage*, *Lesbian Land* and *Shark Bait*, all deal with Sammie's venture into the underground world of female homosexuality. Aware now of her own internalized stereotypes regarding gay men, "I'd already been conned by the stories in my father's porn," she is somewhat better prepared to deal with this new reality, but still has to work through her perceptions and expectations.

In *Shark Bait*, Sammie reflects on the way the lesbian subculture continues to mimic the structure of the dominant society. That is, its tendency to categorize people into strict groups, "Dyke, Femme, Stone Butch, Kiki," and to practice the same kind of judgment and criticism of each other that they themselves so resent in the oppressing culture, "this last said in snide derision." Within these artificial constrictions, Sammie is forced to make a choice about what new identity she will take on.

Sammie's ability to make this choice reflects a survival skill many children growing up in a dysfunctional family unconsciously develop, called the chameleon or co-dependency effect (an essential loss of personal identity as the result of being excessively preoccupied with the needs of others).[56] Burdened with a core sense of being unlovable, the Survivor often struggles with the question, *who do I have to be for you to love me?*

In *Power of Creation*, we witness once again the impact of Abandoned Child Syndrome in the power of Sammie's love addiction — the fusion of sex with love and the confusion of intensity with intimacy. We can also understand her euphoria within the context of abandonment trauma and the desperate need to be connected to a love object.

Flying High, Swinging Low
Pages 147 through 156

Secrets and Lies — sex and love addiction; splitting; ACS, repetition compulsion
Flight — escape compulsion
Hunger — sex addiction
Swing Set — another sexual subculture; "identification with the aggressor," progression of SA
In with the In Crowd — core beliefs surfacing, "it's a man's world"
Sex — survival belief, "beat them at their own game" (sex)
Harnessed Passions — mistrust has generalized to women; secrets maintain individuality; protect against inevitable abandonment

Secrets and Lies reveals that even though Sammie believes that she has finally found "true love" with Kath, she nonetheless continues the pattern of "infidelity" that she began with her husband, Trey. On the surface (consciously) Sammie justifies this as still needing "sex with men on the side," but also recognizes its powerful, compelling nature, "a hunger growling" inside for "the thrill of the hunt, the climatic passion of the kill."

Sammie is experiencing a sex and love addict's unconscious solution to abandonment fears and attachment disorder. Everyone she has ever loved completely (been fully attached to) has emotionally and/or physically abandoned her. When the psyche experiences overwhelming loss and pain, it finds ways to protect itself (defense mechanisms) from pain in the future. No one ever sticks their hand in the fire twice; they learn to put on a mitt.

Sammie is so driven to be in a relationship (Abandoned Child Syndrome), that she races blindly into them; however, once in one, she is driven to protect herself from the inevitable abandonment her unconscious anticipates, by not "putting all of her eggs in one basket." Consequently, she splits her life into two parts — a stable, if unhealthy, home base and a secret sex life — effectively recreating her childhood experience (repetition compulsion).

However, in the last three stanzas of *Secrets and Lies* it appears that Sammie's internal sense of morals is asserting itself, as she realizes that her, "sharp shovel of deception has dug a deep hole in my own heart," with the result that her love for Kath, "leaks out and dies."

In *Flight*, we see that while Sammie realizes on some level that her pattern of running away is a defense against anticipated anger and rejection, she is still powerless to change her behavior. "I run blind to love and deaf to my own heart's screams."

In *Hunger* and *Swing Set*, Sammie finds a sexual playmate that leads her into yet another subculture, where anonymous sex is glorified and there are "no boundaries" on sexual behavior. She readily joins in and "revels in her power." As noted earlier, Sammie's hypersexual behavior is a common symptom of childhood sexual abuse and may reflect the phenomena of identification with the aggressor, a psychological defense mechanism wherein the victim adopts the same values as their captor. By discarding her own sense of appropriate sexual boundaries, Sammie can place herself in the dominant or aggressor role and (subconsciously) attempt to neutralize the traumatic impact of her early incest.

We might also understand Sammie's behavior as reflecting the progressive nature of sex addiction; as the mind develops tolerance to the original level of stimulation, the individual must engage in it more frequently, with increasing levels of intensity, at higher levels of risk and/or in increasingly deviant ways.[57]

In with the In Crowd and *Sex* show us that, while Sammie may consciously try to convince herself she's having a great time, she is not really happy. In these poems, we see more of her internal core beliefs surfacing, "it's a man's world out there" and "you're shit out of luck," if you're not one. Her core belief that men only want sex is evident in *Sex*, as is her survival belief that she has to "seal her heart up tight in skepticism," and "beat them at their own game" (that is, sex).

In *Harnessed Passions*, we see Sammie entering yet another relationship and continuing her practice of "full disclosure" while still keeping secrets. "...there are still some things that I don't share." On some level, she realizes this is a way to protect herself and maintain some sense of individuality. "...after all, isn't that what freedom really means?"

Another Key to Another Body
Pages 159 through 168

Bend or Break – alcohol tolerance; high-risk behavior, DUI; deepening negative self-esteem; self-fulfilling prophecy
Rage – acute fear of anger; flight
Another Key – rapid progression of Sammie's sex and love addiction
Honeymoon – rapid progression of SLA
Just Another Body – SA with Jerry; realizes his emotional abandonment
Familiar Flight – self-perpetuating prophecy; acute fear of anger

In *Bend or Break*, we witness Sammie's growing tolerance for alcohol, "I've been downing shots here since six," and her high-risk behavior in driving while drunk, "how I am able to get home myself God only knows." We also see the continuing emotional damage she causes herself when she is caught in her adultery — both by her current lover and by her "mistress's" partner. Whether it is her attachment disorder that precludes her from taking care of Frankie or a true sacrifice to Frankie's partner, upon letting her go, Sammie deepens her negative self-esteem by identifying as the "cheater [who] will always pay" the price of being alone.

Unknowingly, Sammie is perpetuating a "self-fulfilling prophecy." She believes that she is unlovable; she compulsively races into doomed relationships and, when they end, it confirms her belief that she is unlovable.

Rage demonstrates both Sammie's acute fear of anger, "swept by fear of her return, my father back in female form" and her feelings of guilt over leading a secret double life, even in the context of an open relationship.

In *Another Key*, we see more evidence of the rapid progression of Sammie's love and sex addiction, "paints hardly dry on my last escape when my eyes meet another's across a crowded room." And, in *Honeymoon*, we see that even within the honeymoon stage of a new relationship, she is already distracted by the potential "for kinky sex and wild delights" with a woman she isn't even attracted to, "a drab and stern young-old woman I find of little interest."

In *Just Another Body* we witness Sammie's continuing "addiction" to her second husband, Jerry. For her, the intensity of their sex has always equaled intimacy and love, "for me he's still the best drug out there." But this time she is disturbed by the anonymity of their "hot" sex, "his body's movements rote, his penis there but mind remote" and realizes that, whether because of drugs or schizophrenia, she has once again been emotionally abandoned by a major figure in her life.

In *Familiar Flight*, because Sammie believes she has stayed within the (distorted) boundaries of her "open" relationship with Diane, she feels betrayed by her partner's rage, "stunned and shocked to feel a flash fire of temper flare." Her acute fear of anger triggered, she flees, "still not really knowing just what it is I've done."

Because she herself has no boundaries and has split off her emotional attachment to others from her sexual behavior, it is difficult for Sammie to understand why others can't do the same. However, as her last stanza reveals, on some level, Sammie is beginning to recognize the escape pattern that is emerging in her life, ".... Simply fleeing fear and what seems my destiny/ racing blindly into the night in all too familiar flight."

Other Insight
Pages 171 through 176

Another Door – trauma reenactment/repetition compulsion;
SLA progression and sadomasochism; shame-based self-punish-
ment; repressed rage that needs expression
Partnered In Pain – identification with the aggressor and trau-
ma reenactment/repetition compulsion
Another Broken Heart – porn programming; partial insight;
flight pattern

In *Another Door,* trauma reenactment/repetition compulsion
and the progression of Sammie's sex and love addiction lead
her into a sadomasochistic relationship. Her behavior may be
shame-based, a subconscious effort to "punish" herself for her
bad behavior, as is suggested by the stanza, "...trembling, I stand
with naked soul before my fate."

Sammie may have also reached a breaking point in her ability to
contain her repressed rage, subconsciously seeking a safe outlet
for it, as is suggested by the stanza, "(she) seems still to see a
place where wild rage swells in me."

Partnered In Pain vividly depicts the dynamics of trauma
reenactment and repetition compulsion – the subconscious
drive to recreate an earlier trauma in order to understand or
resolve it in some way. Sammie reveals her dawning awareness
of this process in the stanza, ".... somehow remake the past,
tortured memories recast."

Another Broken Heart represents an important choice point for
Sammie – to continue in a pain-focused relationship (trauma
reenactment) or to reject it. In choosing to reject it, as she did
in *Dishonorable Discharge,* Sammie strengthens her core value
(the core principles that guide our behavior) against hurting others.

However, it is clear that Sammie does not, as yet, have
a conscious understanding of the underlying forces that
drive her own behavior. What we hear instead is a growing

disillusionment with the broken promises of pornography, "Neurotic ecstasy not what I was led to believe...." and a bitter understanding of how, ".... Just another legacy of childhood...." dooms others ".... to a life of pain and perpetual distress," while she herself repeats her own compulsion to flee.

Hitting Bottom, Stepping Up
Pages 179 through 184

Lay Lady Lay – progressive acceleration of addictive pattern
Train Wreck – hitting bottom
Shrink Wrapped – guidance and direction

In keeping with the progressive acceleration of her alcoholism and sex addiction, *Lay Lady Lay* finds Sammie destroying another relationship. Her self-blame, shame and hopelessness regarding her ability to change are powerfully evident in her last stanza:

Not even shocked
I turn away
knowing
there's really nothing
I can say

In *Train Wreck*, it appears that Sammie has hit bottom – has finally reached a point at which she is sick and tired of being sick and tired and knows that she has ".... got to find another way no matter what the cost."

In *Shrink Wrapped*, Sammie realizes that her own "stuff" is ruining her life, as well as that of all the others with whom she tries to be in relationship, "...I break everything that I touch – every life, every heart – always want too much." She finally becomes willing to take action to get help, soon gaining hope that she can change her life by setting out on "a new path of redemption."

ENDNOTES

[1] "Purple Haze," written and recorded by Jimi Hendrix on the album Are You Experienced in 1967.

[2] *"Puff, the Magic Dragon"* is a folk song written by *Leonard Lipton* and *Peter Yarrow*, and made popular by the 60s folk group, *Peter, Paul and Mary*.

[3] *Helter Skelter* written by Paul McCartney, but credited to Lennon–McCartney, recorded by *The Beatles* on the LP The Beatles, better known as *The White Album.*

[4] "It's a Mad, Mad, Mad, Mad World" was a 1963 American comedy film, produced and directed by Stanley Kramer.

[5] "The Letter", a song written by Wayne Carson Thompson, was a #1 hit in 1967 for the Box Tops.

[6] *Behind the Green Door* was a 1972 feature-length pornographic film, widely considered one of the genre's "classic" pictures.

[7] "Lay Lady Lay" is a song written by Bob Dylan and originally released in 1969 on his *Nashville Skyline* album. It quickly became one of his top U.S. hits, peaking at #7 on the *Billboard* Hot 100 that year. It has become a standard and has been covered by numerous bands and artists over the years.

[8] Jaffee, S.R. and Gallop R. Social, emotional, and academic competence among children who have had contact with Child Protective Services: Prevalence and stability estimates. J Am Acad Child Adolesc Psychiatry. 2007 June; 46(6): 757–765. doi: 10.1097/chi.0b013e318040b247.

[9] Bradshaw, John. *Bradshaw on the Family: A Revolutionary Way of Self Discovery.* Deerfield Beach, Florida: Health Communications, 1988; *Bradshaw On: Healing the Shame that Binds You.* Deerfield Beach, Florida: Health Communications, 1988; *Homecoming: Reclaiming and Championing Your Inner Child.* New York, NY: Bantam Books. 1990. PBS Television series, 1982-95.

[10] Goldstein, Kurt. *The Organism: A Holistic Approach to Biology Derived from Pathological Data in Man*, New York: Zone Books, 1939/1995, as cited in Modell, Arnold H.. The Private Self, Cambridge, MA: Harvard University Press, 1993, p 44; Maslow, A. H. Notes on being-psychology. *Journal of Humanistic Psychology*, 2, 1962, 47-71. doi:10.1177/002216786200200205

[11] Thompson, Kate. "Journal therapy writing as a therapeutic tool." Trans. Array Writing Cures: an introductory handbook of writing in counseling and therapy. Gillie Bolton, Stephanie Howlett, Colin Lago and Jeannie K. Wright. New York City: Brunner-Routledge, 2004. 72-84.

[12] Glaser, D. Emotional abuse and neglect (psychological maltreatment): A conceptual framework. *Child Abuse & Neglect*, 26 (2002): 697-714.

[13] Dutton, D. G., & Painter, S. L. (1981). Traumatic Bonding: The development of emotional attachments in battered women and other relationships of intermittent abuse. *Victimology: An International Journal*, 7(4), 139-155.

[14] Herman, Judith, *Father-Daughter Incest*, Harvard University Press, 2000 (Previous ed.: 1981), p. 72.

[15] Whitfield, Charles. Healing the Child Within. Health Communications, Inc. 1987.

[16] Hurley, Dorothy H. Spiritual Impact of Childhood Sexual Abuse, *Journal of Religion & Abuse*, 6:2 (2004): 81-101, p21; DOI: 10.1300/J154v06n02_05; Ganje-Fling, M. and McCarthy, P., "Impact of Childhood Sexual Abuse on Client Spiritual Development: Counseling Implications". *Journal of Counseling & Development*, 74:3 (1996): 253-9.

[17] Ibid

[18] Dube, S.R., Anda, R.F., Whitfield, C.L., Brown, D.W., Felitti, V.J., Dong, M., Giles, W.H.. Long-term consequences of childhood sexual abuse by gender of victim. Am J Prev Med. 2005 Jun;28(5):430-8.

[19] National Vital Statistics Report, Vol. 61, No. 4, May 8, 2013, p 90.

[20] National Alliance on Mental Illness, "Fact Sheet on Dissociative Disorders", retrieved 02/20/14. *http://www.nami.org/Content/ NavigationMenu/Inform_Yourself/About_Mental_Illness/By_Illness/ Dissociative_Disorders.htm)*

[21] Ibid

[22] Malchiodi, C. (Ed.). *Handbook of Art Therapy*. New York:Guilford Press, 2003, p 1.

[23] Malchiodi, C., Trauma-Informed Expressive Arts Therapy, Psychology Today, March 6, 2012. http://www.psychologytoday.com/blog/the-healing-arts/201203/trauma-informed-expressive-arts-therapy

[24] Browne, A. & Finkelhor, D. (1986). Impact of child sexual abuse: A review of the research. *Psychological Bulletin*, 99, 66-77.

[25] Karakurt, G. and K. E. Silver. Therapy for Childhood Sexual Abuse Survivors Using Attachment and Family Systems Theory Orientations. *The Am. J.of Family Therapy*, 42:79–91, 2014.

[26] Hazan. C. and Shaver, P. R. Romantic love conceptualized as an attachment process. *Journal of Personality and Social Psychology* . 52:3 (1987): 511–24, p 512.

[27] Cavanagh-Johnson, T. Assessment of sexual behavior problems in pre-school aged and latency-aged children. *Sexual and Gender Identity Disorders*, 2 (1993): 431–449; Dubowitz, H., Black, M., Harrington, D., & Verschoore, A. A follow up study of behavior problems associated with child sexual abuse. *Child Abuse & Neglect*, 17 (1993): 743–754; Friedrich, W. N. Sexual victimization and sexual behavior in children: A review of recent literature. *Child Abuse & Neglect*, 17 (1993): 59–66.

[28] Martin, B. (2006). Fight or Flight. *Psych Central*. Retrieved on February 18, 2014, from http://psychcentral.com/lib/fight-or-flight/00030

[29] Fergusson, D. M., Horwood, L. J. and Lynskey, M. T. Childhood sexual abuse, adolescent sexual behaviors and sexual revictimization. *Child Abuse & Neglect*, 21:8 (1997): 789-803; Noll, J. G., Trickett, P. K. and Putnam, F. W. A prospective investigation of the impact of

childhood sexual abuse on the development of sexuality. *Journal of Consulting and Clinical Psychology*, 71:3 (2003): 575-587.

[30] Kirby, D., Lepore, G. and Ryan, J. Sexual risk and protective factors: Factors affecting teen sexual behavior, pregnancy, childbearing, and sexually transmitted disease. Washington, DC: The National Campaign to Prevent Teen Pregnancy (2005).

[31] Davis, K.E. and G.N. Braucht. *Exposure to Pornography, Character and Sexual Deviance*, Technical Reports of the Commission on Obscenity and Pornography, 1970, p7; Carnes, P. Don't Call It Love: Recovery from Sexual Addictions, New York: Bantam, 1991; Stephen J. Kavanagh, *Protecting Children in Cyberspace* . Springfield, VA: Behavioral Psychotherapy Center, 1997, 58-59. Cline, V.B. *Pornography's Effects on Adults and Children*, New York: Morality in Media, 1990, p11; Garcia, L.T. Exposure to Pornography and Attitudes about Women and Rape: A Correlative Study, AG 22, 1986, 382-83; Bergman, J., "The Influence of Pornography on Sexual Development: Three Case Histories," *Family Therapy IX*, no. 3 (1982): 265.

[32] Cline, V.P., *Pornography's Effects on Adults and Children*, 11.

[33] Reinert, D. F. and C. E. Smith. Childhood sexual abuse and female spiritual development. *Counseling and Values*, 41:235–45 (1997).

[34] Gold, J., Wolan Sullivan, M. and Lewis, M. The relation between abuse and violent delinquency: The conversion of shame to blame in juvenile offenders. *Child Abuse & Neglect*, 35(7), 459–467 (2011).

[35] Slade E.P., Wissow, L.S. The influence of childhood maltreatment on adolescents' academic performance. Economics of Education Review. 2007; 26(5): 604–614.

[36] van der Kolk, B.A. "The Compulsion to Repeat the Trauma Re-enactment, Revictimization, and Masochism." *Psychiatric Clinics of North America*, 12:2 (1989) 389-411.

[37] Coohey, C., and Braun, N. Toward an integrated framework for understanding child physical abuse. *Child Abuse & Neglect*. 21 (1997): 1081-1094.

[38] Finkelhor, D. & Browne, A. The traumatic impact of child sexual abuse: A conceptualization. American Journal of Orthopsychiatry, 55:4, (1985): 530-541.

[39] Ibid, 25.

[40] Bolger, K. E., & Patterson, C. J. Developmental pathways from child maltreatment to peer rejection. *Child Development*, 72:2 (2001): 549–568.

[41] McDougall, P., Hymel, S., Vaillancourt, T., & Mercer, L. The consequences of childhood rejection, in M. R. Leary (Ed.), *Interpersonal rejection*. New York, NY: Oxford University Press, 2001, 213-247, as cited in Lev-Wiesel, R.; Sternberg, R. Victimized at Home Revictimized by Peers: Domestic Child Abuse a Risk Factor in Social Rejection, *Child & Adolescent Social Work Journal*. 29:3 (2012): 203-220. DOI: 10.1007/s10560-012-0258-0

[42] van der Kolk (1989).

[43] Felitti, V. J. and Anda, R. The relationship of adverse childhood experiences to adult medical disease, psychiatric disorders, and sexual behavior: Implications for healthcare, in R. Lanius, R., Vermetten, E. and Pain, C. (Eds.), *The hidden epidemic: The impact of early life trauma on health and disease*. 2009. Retrieved from http://www.acestudy.org/yahoo_site_admin/assets/ docs/LaniusVermetten_FINAL_8-26-09.12892303.pdf.

[44] Maltby, L.E. and Hall, T.W. Trauma, Attachment, and Spirituality: A Case Study. *Journal of Psychology & Theology*. 40 (2012) 302-312 p 302.

[45] Griffin-Shelley, E. *Adolescent Sex and Love Addicts*, New York: Praeger Publishers, 1994, 17; Carnes, Patrick, P. *Out of the Shadows: Understanding Sexual Addiction*. Minneapolis, MN: CompCare Publications. 1983; Carnes, P. *Contrary to Love: Helping the Sexual Addict*. Minneapolis, MN: CompCare Publications, 1989; Covington, S. and Beckett, L. *Leaving the Enchanted Forest: The Path from Relationship Addiction to Intimacy*. New York: Harper & Row, 1988; Mellody, P., Wells A. and Miller, J. K. *Facing Love Addiction: Giving Yourself the Power to Change the Way You Love*. San Francisco, CA: Harper, 1992.

[46] Herman, J. L. Father-daughter incest. Cambridge, MA: Harvard University Press, 1981; Herman, J. L. and Lewis, H. B. Anger in the mother-daughter relationship, 1986, in T. Bernay and Cantor, D.W. (Eds.), *The psychology of today's woman: New Psychoanalytic visions*.

Hillsdale, NJ: Analytic Press; Rosenthal, P. A. and Doherty, M. B. Psychodynamics of delinquent girls rage and violence directed toward mother. *Adolescent Psychiatry,* 12 (1985): 281-289.

[47] Arata, C. M. Child sexual abuse and sexual revictimization. *Clinical Psychology: Science & Practice*, 9 (2002):135–164.

[48] Garssen, B. Repression: Finding Our Way in the Maze of Concepts. *J Behav Med.* 30 (2007)(6): 471–481.

[49] Walker, M. D., Hernandez, A. M. and Davey, M. Childhood Sexual Abuse and Adult Sexual Identity Formation: Intersection of Gender, Race, and Sexual Orientation. *American Journal of Family Therapy.* 40:5 (2012) 385-398, 14 DOI: 10.1080/01926187.2011.627318.

[50] Balsam, K. F. Trauma, stress, and resilience among sexual minority women: Rising like the phoenix. *Journal of Lesbian Studies,* 7, (2003): 1–8; Dietz, C. Working with lesbian, gay, bisexual and transgendered abuse survivors. *Journal of Progressive Human Services,* 12, (2001): 27–49; Morris, J., & Balsam, K. F. Lesbian and bisexual women's experiences of victimization: Mental health, revictimization, and sexual identity development. *Journal of Lesbian Studies,* 7 (2003): 67–85. Russell, J. D., Jones, R. A., Barclay, K. and Anderson, M. Managing transference and countertransference in the treatment of gay, lesbian and bisexual of childhood sexual abuse. *Journal of Gay & Lesbian Mental Health*, 12 (2008) 227–243.

[51] Morris, J. F., & Balsam, K. F. Lesbian and bisexual women's experiences of victimization: Mental health, revictimization, and sexual identity development. *Journal of Lesbian Studies*, 7 (2003) 67–85; Paul J., Cantania, J., Pollack, L., & Stall, R. Understanding childhood sexual abuse as a predictor of sexual risk taking among men who have sex with men: The urban men's health study. *Child Abuse & Neglect*, 25 (2001) 557–584; Saewyc, E. M., Skay, C. L, Pettingell, S. L, Reis, E. A., Bearinger, L., Resnick, M., Combs, L. Hazards of stigma: The sexual and physical abuse of gay, lesbian, and bisexual adolescents in the United States and Canada. *Child Welfare*, 85. (2006) 195–213.

[52] Carnes, Patrick, *Sexual Anorexia : Overcoming Sexual Self-Hatred*, Hazelden, 1997.

[53] Carnes, Patrick J. The case for sexual anorexia: An interim report on 144 patients with sexual disorders. "Sexual Addiction & Compulsivity 5".(4): 293–309. (1998).

[54] Mellody, P., Miller, A.W. and K. Miller, *Facing Love Addiction*, HarperCollins, 1992.

[55] Hardy, Kenneth V., Reclaiming Children & Youth. Spring 2013, Vol. 22 Issue 1, 26.

[56] Mellody, P., Miller, A.W., and Miller, J.K. *Facing Codependence: What It Is, Where It Comes from, How It Sabotages Our Lives*, HarperOne, 2003.

[57] *Don't Call It Love: Recovery From Sexual Addiction*, Bantam (reprint edition), 1992.

National Association of Adult Survivors of Child Abuse
http://www.naasca.org/

Adult Children of Alcoholics
World Service Organization, Inc. (ACA WSO)
P.O.Box 3216
Torrance CA 90510
http://www.adultchildren.org/

http://www.isurvive.org/
Offers resources and forums

Survivors of Incest Anonymous (SIA)
World Service Office
P.O. Box 190
Benson , MD 21018-9998
http://www.siawso.org/
http://www.ascasupport.org/

Incest Survivors Anonymous (ISA)
http://www.lafn.org/medical/isa/home.html
Self-help, mutual-help twelve-step support groups for survivors. For
groups & meeting information and literature write them, (specify you
are a survivor) or call.
P.O. Box 17245
Long Beach, CA. 90807-7245

Male Survivor
PMB 103
5505 Connecticut Avenue, NW
Washington , DC 20015-2601
Toll-Free: 1-800-738-4181
http://www.malesurvivor.org/

Survivors Network of those Abused by Priests- SNAP
http://www.snapnetwork.org/
SNAP provides support and knowledge to all victims of clergy abuse and advocates helping ensure that in future generations, children will be safe. (U.S. & Canada)
PO Box 6416
Chicago, IL 60680-6416

ASCA (Adult Survivors of Child Abuse) by the Morris Center
http://www.ascasupport.org/
The Morris Center
P.O. Box 14477
San Francisco, CA 94114

BOOKS

Bass, Ellen & Davis, Laura: *The Courage to Heal: A Guide for Women Survivors of Child Sexual Abuse,* Vermilion; new edition, 2002; *The Courage to Heal Workbook*, Harper Perennial, 1990.

Bradshaw, John: Healing the Shame that Binds You, Health Communications, 1988; Homecoming: Reclaiming and Championing Your Inner Child; Family Secrets - The Path to Self-Acceptance and Reunion, Little, Brown Book Group, 1991. All books by this author are recommended.

Bloomfield, Harold H: Making Peace with Your Parents, Random House, 1983.
Forward, Susan: Toxic Parents: Overcoming Their Hurtful Legacy and Reclaiming Your Life, Bantam, 2nd Revised edition, 2002.

Fromm, Eric: The Art of Loving, Harper Perennial Modern Classics, 2006.
Gil, Eliana: Outgrowing the Pain, Dell, Reissue edition, 1988.

Herman, Judith: Trauma and Recovery: The aftermath of violence from domestic abuse to political terror, Basic Books, Reprint edition, 1997; Father-Daughter Incest, Basic Books, 1997.

Maltz, Wendy: The Sexual Healing Journey: A Guide for Survivors of Sexual Abuse, William Morrow Paperbacks, 3 Rev Upd edition, 2012.

Matsakis, Aphrodite: I Can't Get Over It, A Handbook for Trauma Survivors, New Harbinger Publications, 2nd Revised edition, 1996.

Miller, Alice: Thou Shalt Not Be Aware: Society's Betrayal of the Child. Farrar, Straus and Giroux, 1998; For Your Own Good: Hidden Cruelty in Child-rearing and the Roots of Violence, Farrar, Straus and Giroux, 3rd edition, 2002. All books by this author are recommended.

Spear, Joan: Can I Trust My Memory? – A handbook for survivors with partial or no memories of childhood sexual abuse, Hazelden, 1992.

Whitfield, Charles: Healing The Child Within: Discovery and Recovery for Adult Children of Dysfunctional Families, Health Communications, Inc., 1987; A Gift to Myself: A Personal Workbook and Guide to Healing the Child Within, Health Communications, Inc., 1990.

MEN

Grubman-Black, Stephen: Broken Boys/Mending Men, The Blackburn Press, 2002.

Hunter, Mic: Abused Boys: The Neglected Victims of Sexual Abuse, Ballantine Books, 1990.

Lew, Mike: Victims No Longer: Men Recovering from Incest and Other Sexual Child Abuse, Harper Collins, 1988.

Sanders, Timothy: Male Survivors: 12-Setp Recovery Program for Survivors of Childhood Sexual Abuse, Crossing Pr, 1991.

PARTNERS

Barshinger, Clark, Lojan La Rowe, and Andres Tapia: Haunted Marriage: Overcoming the Ghosts of Your Spouse's Childhood Abuse, Intervarsity Pr., 1995.

Davis, Laura: Allies in Healing: When the Person You Love Was Sexually Abused as a Child, William Morrow Paperbacks, 1991.

Engel, Beverly: Partners in Recovery, Lowell House, 1991.
Gil, Eliana: Outgrowing the Pain Together, Dell, 1992.
Cameron, Grant: What about me? A Guide for Men Helping Female Partners Deal with Childhood Sexual Abuse, Creative Bound, 6th edition, 1994.

Graber, Ken: Ghosts in the Bedroom: A Guide for the Partners of Incest Survivors, Health Communications, Inc., 1991.

Matsakis, Aphrodite: Trust After Trauma: A Guide to Relationships for Survivors and Those Who Love Them, New Harbinger Publications, 1998.

Haines, Staci: The Survivor's Guide to Sex: How to Have an Empowered Sex Life After Child Sexual Abuse, Cleis Press, 1999.

CHILDREN

Holmes, Margaret. A Terrible Thing Happened, Magination Pr, 2000.

McKinnon, Marjorie: REPAIR for Kids, Loving Healing Press, 2008.

McKinnon, Marjorie, Michal Splho and Sharon Wallace, REPAIR For Teens: A Program for Recovery, Loving Healing Press, 2012.

Satullo, Jane and Russell Bradway: It Happens to Boys, Too, Rape Crisis Center of the Berkshires Press, 1987.

ABOUT DR. ELAINE BRADY

Elaine Brady, Ph.D. MFT, CAS, CSAT-S is the founder and Executive Director of Net Worth Recovery, Inc., an Internet and Sex Addiction treatment center located in San Jose, CA. Dr. Brady is a frequent presenter and keynote speaker at local and national conferences, conducts staff trainings for local school districts and is an adjunct professor at several Santa Clara County colleges. She specializes in topics relating to Internet Addiction in Adults and Children; Cyberbullying; Internet Sex Offenders; Gaming Addiction and Cybersex Addiction.

She is widely published in numerous trade journals such as the Family Law News; New Times, National Council on Alcoholism and Drug Dependence; the California Psychologist and the Santa Clara Valley CAMFT News. Some of her featured articles have included, "Hit and Run on the Superhighway of Love" (with Lynne Yates-Carter, Esq.), "Internet Infidelity", and "Tiger Woods' Path through Sex Addiction".

Dr. Brady has appeared on CBS-5 and NBC-11 covering relevant topics like "Craigslist's Adult Postings," "Potville," and the "Gambling Opt-out Program." She has been a guest speaker on the Gil Cross Talk 910 Radio show (KKSF-AM) discussing her work with online gaming and pornography addiction.

Dr. Brady has served as an expert witness in numerous court cases and has made several presentations to the Santa Clara County Bar Association; the Association of Certified Family Law Specialists; the California Coalition on Sexual Offending, the Women's Association for Addiction Treatment; CONCERN- EAP; Sequoia Center and the Child & Family Counseling Group.

Dr. Brady lives in Northern California where, in addition to directing her treatment center, she is working on the sequel to Forged in Fire/Girl on Fire entitled, Forged in Fire/Redemption. She is also preparing to raft the Grand Canyon and continuing to add to her ever-expanding Wizard of Oz collection.